PRAISES FOR TRANSFORM MY THINKING, GOD

What a timely, God initiated, God endorsed study. Elizabeth Mahusay, a woman who knows and loves the scriptures addresses the often confused thought patterns that dominate the thinking of today's woman. As she unpacks the life changing truths in the book of Philippians, I believe women will be released from the bondage of wrong thinking and come alive to both the vision God has of them and for them. Without hesitation I would encourage every woman to carefully study and apply the principles of this transformational study.

Debbie Weisemann
Minister of Outreach
Bell Shoals Baptist Church

If you were watching TV, but could not turn it off, what would you do? Change channels! That's what Elizabeth Mahusay counsels in her new book, *Transform My Thinking, God*. Her simple but profound directive is to switch the focus of our minds to Him. All who read these pages will find remarkable guidance to learn how to think God's thoughts.

Jimmy Draper
President Emeritus
LifeWay Christian Resources

In her powerful study *Transform My Thinking, God*, Elizabeth shows us how we can become people of God who bring joy to churches, pastors, families, friends, and ourselves! Her study is desperately needed to counter the culture around us, because it's true, "Where the mind goes, the body and heart will follow." I have led many Bible studies, from many sources. I believe *Transform My Thinking, God* will greatly impact the lives of many people.

Gail Williams
Women's Bible Study Teacher
Cottonwood Creek Church

Elizabeth Mahusay's Bible study, *Transform My Thinking, God,* is excellent! Last year, I led 23 women with a broad range of ages, backgrounds, and biblical knowledge, through Elizabeth's study. We loved it! It not only aided us in understanding God's word and promises, but led us to transform our thinking and change our actions and habits. Simply, it put our feet to the fire. It has been a year since we completed the study, yet I find myself often reflecting on its principles.

Kathi Pfahl
Women's Bible Study Leader, Willard Christian Reformed Church
Executive Director, Premier Designs Jewelry

Elizabeth's *Transform My Thinking, God* study changed my life! It sounds like an exaggeration, but this study changed the trajectory of my thinking in all areas of my life. I can now filter my thoughts through the lens of God's truths. My relationship with the Lord has grown by leaps and bounds. God gave Elizabeth the gift of helping readers identify the lies of the enemy, and how to lean into God's word to gain a Christ-centered mentality. I recommend this study to everyone. It's transformational!

Tiffany Snow
Wife and mom of three

The *Transform My Thinking, God* study by Elizabeth Mahusay is one of the best Bible studies I've ever taken. The comprehensive way that Elizabeth breaks down the Book of Philippians and conveys the truth of God's Word is timely and relevant. The six "Mindset" principles challenged me to take my thought life captive, and convicted me to redirect my thinking to God's Word, His promises, and what He desires for me.

Elizabeth Licht
Wife, mother, business owner

Transform
My Thinking,
GOD

Transform My Thinking, GOD

6 Principles to Beat Negative Thinking and Build the Life You Want

A Study of the Book of Philippians

ELIZABETH B MAHUSAY

Transform My Thinking, God:
6 Principles to Beat Negative Thinking and Build the Life You Want

Copyright © 2018 Elizabeth B. Mahusay

All rights reserved.

Editor: Sheri A. Bell

Printed in the United States of America

Published by Author Academy Elite
PO BOX 43
Powell, Ohio 43035
www.AuthorAcademyElite.com

ISBN: 978-1-64085-296-9 Paperback
ISBN: 978-1-64085-297-6 Hardback

Library of Congress Control Number: 2018942474

Dedication

My parents —

To Annie and Edward Bethel, for bringing me to church from early childhood and training me up in the way I should go, for praying for me even when I was wayward, for your love and support of me no matter the endeavor.

To Betty and Cliff Bennett, for instilling in me a love for travel and time with family, for encouraging me to be an avid reader and diligent student, for your love especially through my teenage years, for your constant encouragement.

My sons —

To Anthony, for your winsome smile and genuine interest in what is happening in my life, for your deep thinking, for your "punny" disposition.

To Samuel, for your warm and inviting smile, for your sensitive spirit, for your ability to find the positive regardless of the circumstances.

My husband, best friend, partner in life —

To Fred, for your endless pursuit of me since high school, for your uncanny way of making me laugh, for your constant encouragement to pursue God's best, for your willingness to pray for me and over me, for your commitment to love me as Christ loved the church, for your steadfast belief that this published study would become a reality.

CONTENTS

Foreword   xi

Author's Note   xiii

Acknowledgements   xv

Study Notes and Suggestions   1

Week 1 GOSPEL MINDSET
   Being Others-centered in a Self-centered World   2

Week 2 NO MATTER WHAT MINDSET
   Focus on the Cross More Than Your Circumstances   24

Week 3 CHRIST-LIKE EVERYDAY MINDSET
   Humbly Decrease so That Christ Can Increase   44

Week 4 HEAVEN-FOCUSED MINDSET
   Cultivate There and Then Thinking and Make Your Dash Count   70

Week 5 INTENTIONALITY AND GOD-CONFIDENCE
MINDSET

    5 Steps to Retrain Your Brain   98

GOD-CONFIDENCE MINDSET   119

God-Confidence Mindset LISTENING GUIDE

    Anchor Your Mind in God's Power, Purpose, and Provision   126

Appendix   131

Endnotes and Resources   132

About the Author   135

FOREWORD

I was in attendance at the very first Bible study Elizabeth taught, which happen to be on Philippians. Her spiritual growth from then to present day is apparent. Through the years I have watched her personally grow through each of the 6 Mindsets identified in *Transform My Thinking, God*, which makes her uniquely qualified in writing this Bible study.

I have had the privilege of watching God transform Elizabeth's thinking as she has tackled the biblical truths Paul shares with us in Philippians. At first she tried to tackle these truths in her own strength. But then, through the power of the Holy Spirit, Elizabeth slowly relinquished control and learned to rely on and trust the Lord for all things.

Elizabeth's increased love for the Lord, the Word, the lost, coupled with her faith and the urgency to share the Gospel, are all additions to her spiritual growth repertoire.

My prayer for her is that she continually relies on Him, and that she always remembers 1 Corinthians 10:12. My prayer for you, dear reader, as you embark on the *Transform My Thinking, God* study, is that you too will choose to surrender it all to the One who holds your future.

In His Service
Theresa L. Miller

2018

A NOTE FROM ELIZABETH

Dear Woman of God,

The book of Philippians is exceptionally personal to me because God has used it in such a powerful way in my life. I first studied it in early 2004. In 2006, I wrote my very first women's Bible study based on Philippians, which I titled *Make My Joy Complete*. I was scared out of mind to undertake the task. I was riddled with fear that I would fail or get it wrong, and rather than hear God say, "Well done," I would hear Him say, "What were you thinking?"

God graciously carried me through that four-week study, and in the years that have followed, He has taught me much. As we embark on the study of God's Word, my prayer for you is that your mind openly receives it. Soften your heart to the truths God conveys to you through His Word. Yield to the Spirit of God for the accomplishment of His will for you.

Over our next six weeks together, we will look at Paul and how his thinking ensured that he lived a life that furthered the Gospel. We will study six different principles — which I call Mindsets — that God can use to cultivate our transformed thinking. Our aim is to deepen our understanding of God and how He empowers us to act on these Mindsets so that we daily magnify Christ.

Transformed thinking does not happen overnight, ladies. It is a process. The thought patterns that have brought us to the present did not get here overnight, nor will they change overnight. Just like the butterfly must struggle to break free from the cocoon in order to fly, I encourage you to embrace the struggle for right thinking. Ask God to strengthen the wings of your heart and mind with His truth. Allow Him to transform your old ways of thinking so you can take flight and enjoy the freedom of His best for you.

I am praying for you, Sisters! I look forward to hearing how God's Word is transforming your thinking.

Serving in love,

Elizabeth

ACKNOWLEDGEMENTS

Transform My Thinking, God is in your hands today because of God's grace in my own journey of transformed thinking. God placed people in my life to encourage me to walk by faith. He used others to challenge my pride, and others to pray for me and walk alongside of me. Most importantly God used His Word to bring freedom in my life and His Spirit to guide me in the writing process.

I am thankful for Debbie Weissmann who believed in me and gave me opportunities to grow as a women's Bible Study teacher. I will always remember her telling me to step up to the podium with a blank page and allow God to speak.

I am thankful for Gayle Owens who taught me homiletics, helped me write my first study guide, and instilled in me a love for God's Word. I will always remember her telling me not to compare myself to others and that God can supernaturally make what I say exactly what the hearer needs.

I am thankful for Theresa Miller and our conversations on her back patio. She introduced me to Oswald Chambers, encouraged me through scripture, and left her "Theresa-isms" indelibly marked on my mind. She has always spoken the truth in love, and I am better for it. Her declaration, "Elizabeth, those ladies got a lot of Joshua but none of you" was the beginning of my learning to be transparent. I will always remember her sharing 1 Corinthians 10:12-13 with me and her admonition to be humble.

I am thankful for all the women who have taken this study prior to publishing. Their timely notes and messages expressing gratitude for the study encouraged and strengthened me to press forward in the publishing process. I will always remember the first time I read, "Your study changed my life!"

I am thankful for my family and friends that have loved me, inspired me, and expressed their belief in my gift of teaching. We have laughed together, cried together, raised our children together, and made lots of memories together. I will always remember the difference their prayers have made in my journey.

I am thankful for Sheri A. Bell, writer and editor extraordinaire. Her passion for the written word and meticulousness in editing have been invaluable to me. She is gifted with the ability to ensure that what I am thinking is accurately communicated to the reader. I will always remember her challenge to dig deeper and give more of myself.

I am thankful for Betty, Yoana, and Sharen, for proofreading the manuscript. Their edits, suggestions, and attention to the details were so helpful. I will always remember their sacrifice of time in making this the best study possible.

I am so thankful for Fred, my husband, for his constant encouragement. He sacrificed often to allow space in my schedule to write. His pursuit of God, his love of others, and his leadership in our home inspire me. I will always remember the wet willy that started it all. After all these years, I am still smiling.

STUDY NOTES AND SUGGESTIONS

I studied numerous sources while writing this text, including multiple Philippians commentaries and *Strong's Exhaustive Bible Concordance*. There is a complete Resource list in the back of the book, should you want to reference any as part of your daily study. Here are other helpful suggestions:

1. The New King James Version (NKJV) is the version used in the writing of this study guide. You may find it easier to use that version as you complete your homework.

2. Visit www.elizabethmahusay.com to gain access to the weekly videos, for which there are listening guides at the beginning of each week of homework.

3. Use the journaling opportunities at the end of each day to consider what you are thinking. Do not overanalyze your thoughts. Rather, record the first thoughts that come to mind. You can always go back and add more as the Lord brings additional thoughts to mind.

4. Develop a scripture memory plan. At a minimum, make it your goal to memorize a verse that speaks to you. Or you might choose to memorize a larger section, if not an entire chapter. If memorization is easy for you, go for the gold: memorize the entire book of Philippians.

GOSPEL MINDSET

LISTENING GUIDE
Philippians 1:1-11

THREE IMPORTANT FACTS ABOUT THOUGHTS:

1. Thoughts are _____ (to our Mindset).

2. Thoughts are _____.

3. Thoughts are _____.

G:

O:

S:

P:

E:

L:

Gospel
MINDSET

GOSPEL MINDSET
Day 1

This week you'll study and think about the first half of Philippians 1. My heart's desire is that you will consider how to be other's centered in a self-centered world. Visit www.elizabethmahusay.com to access and watch the Gospel Mindset video and fill in the listening guide.

READ THE ENTIRE BOOK OF PHILIPPIANS. (DON'T WORRY; IT'S ONLY FOUR CHAPTERS!)

Philippians is a joyful letter, written by Paul, to the believers in the church at Philippi. The setting: Paul is imprisoned in a dank Roman cell, chained to a guard 24/7, as he awaits trial. Paul can't preach in public, but he is able to receive visitors and continues to share the Gospel. As Paul enjoys a deep relationship with the Philippian church, its members are a source of great encouragement to him during his imprisonment. Paul's letter addresses his love for them, thanks them for their financial support, and exhorts them to unity and faithfulness.

FOCUS ON CHAPTER 1:1-2.

Paul begins by calling himself a bondservant of Jesus Christ. The term comes from the Greek word *doulos*, which describes a person owned by someone else and dependent on that person. When used in the New Testament to describe a believer's relationship to Jesus Christ, *doulos* describes willing, determined, and devoted service. Paul is single-minded in his devotion to Christ, and he wants to encourage the Philippian believers to have the same mindset. He knows the impact it can have in furthering the Gospel.

1. Would you describe yourself as a bondservant of Jesus Christ? What are the benefits of being a bondservant of Jesus Christ?

2. What areas of your life most challenge you to depend on Jesus? Why?

I tend toward being an independent, self-sufficient, "get-er-done" kind of woman. To be dependent on anyone, *especially* God, is difficult for me. Yet,

> PEACE CAN ONLY GROW OUT OF A PERSONAL RESPONSE TO GOD'S GRACE.

my independence and self-sufficiency get me into so much trouble when I create my plans and then ask God to bless them. Note that Paul does not commend self-sufficiency to the Philippian believers. Instead, he declares "grace to you and peace from God our Father and the Lord Jesus Christ" (Philippians 1:2). The placement of peace second is significant. *Peace can only grow out of a personal response to God's grace.*

3. Define grace in your own words.

I think of grace as receiving that which I do not deserve. The grace Paul references here is the unmerited favor of God, expressed through Jesus' death on the cross, His burial, and His resurrection to the right hand of God in order to secure our eternal salvation. Whew! That is a mouthful! Unmerited means undeserved. Indeed, we do not deserve God's grace. We cannot be enough, do enough, say enough, or give enough to deserve God's grace, yet He gives it to us! Let that truth sink into your mind.

4. Knowing that God gives us what we don't deserve, what thoughts should we have about God?

5. Since God gives us what we don't deserve, why do you think it is so hard to extend grace to people God places in our lives?

READ EPHESIANS 2:8-9.

6. List what you read are important components of salvation.

These verses clearly state that salvation is by grace through faith. The Good News of salvation is available to all through Jesus Christ. When we accept that grace, *then* God grants us peace. Not peace as the world defines it, but the peace of knowing our eternity is secure in Christ Jesus. That is good news worth sharing! We need a Gospel Mindset to be effective and consistent in sharing that Good News. Paul, as the author of a large portion of the New Testament, models a Gospel Mindset.

I shared earlier about my self-sufficiency. I am not sure when I began to think that I had to have it all together, but that thought led me to behave in ways that made the Gospel less attractive to my non-Christian friends, coworkers, and even to the ladies with whom I was studying God's Word. I mean after all, who can relate to someone who projects that she is perfect, when we all know we are imperfect? As I reflect back, people saw too much of me, and not enough of Jesus! During that season of my life, I shared the Gospel very little.

7. Rate yourself on a scale of 1 to 10 (1 being unlikely and 10 being very likely) of how likely you are to share the Gospel with others.

_____

Spend time journaling some of the thoughts you believe keep you from freely sharing the Gospel.

GOSPEL MINDSET
Day 2

READ PHILIPPIANS 1:1-5.

Paul is so thankful. In verse three, we see him thanking "my God" every time he remembers the Philippians. He would have surely remembered all that was recorded in Acts 16. Highlights from that chapter: Lydia, who heard Paul preach and responded; the slave girl, out of whom Paul cast the demon (which resulted in his imprisonment by her masters); the jailer's salvation, and the fact that the Philippian church is the only church supporting him financially. As these remembrances entered his mind, Paul thanks God, which prompts him to keep the church in prayer. What a wonderful example of walking in the Spirit that Paul shares in Galatians 5:16-18, 22-26.

When we are controlled by the Holy Spirit, we remember and focus on the goodness, kindness, and successes of others—while looking past their weaknesses and shortcomings.

1. Are you characterized by remembering and dwelling on the good of others, or the bad?

I have definitely struggled with focusing on the negatives in others over the years. As God has been transforming my thoughts, I have learned to say, "It takes one to know one." What I mean by this is that if I see a negative in someone, it is because I have or have had that very trait within myself at some point! Ladies, that is a stinging truth for me! But it helps to remind me that God always shows me grace, and I should extend that same grace to others. I always do a better job of extending grace when I *pray* more for people and *talk less* about people.

Paul teaches us a great deal about prayer in verse four. The word prayer has a basic meaning of a request, plea, or supplication addressed to God (Romans 10:1, Hebrews 5:7, I Peter 3:12). This does not suggest that Paul prays for the Philippians all day every day, but it does mean that anytime he thinks about them, he prays specifically for them "with joy." Paul is fully aware of his big picture here: confinement to a guard, unable to preach publicly, fellow teachers and preachers intending to cause him distress, believers squabbling within the church, and the unknown outcome (life or death) of his trial. Paul has joy despite these things, because he is single-minded in proclaiming the Gospel.

We can, then, conclude that such single-mindedness in our thinking can produce joy that leads to our actively praying for the body of Christ. This is a great example of how thought lays the foundation for attitudes, which we express through our behavior. Having a Gospel Mindset compels us to pray.

2. Are there persons you are actively praying for right now? What are you asking God to do in their lives?

In verse five we read that Paul also is joyful for the Philippians' "participation in the Gospel from the first day until now." The meaning of participation is commonly rendered as "fellowship" or "communion," and has the root meaning of "sharing something in common." The Philippians are active partners with Paul in spreading the Good News of salvation. As Bible commentator John MacArthur writes, "They had faithfully served with him in their church, proclaimed the Gospel with him, worshiped and prayed with him, and defended the faith with him. They had abundantly shared their material resources with him over and over again. They had tirelessly and selflessly been in partnership with him *from the first day until now*, over a period of several years."[1]

3. How are you participating in sharing the Gospel through your local church?

4. How has your participation changed the way you think about God? About your church? About the importance of salvation for others?

Journal your thoughts on why most churchgoers believe their pastor and other staff members are primarily responsible for sharing the Gospel.

_____

_____

_____

_____

_____

_____

_____

_____

GOSPEL MINDSET
Day 3

READ PHILIPPIANS 1:1-8.

In the video lesson for the Gospel Mindset, I shared five statements that have been difference-makers in my life. Reading 2 Corinthians 1:18-20 helps us to

_____

"GOD CAN DO WHAT HE SAYS HE CAN DO!"

_____

better understand one of the statements: *"God can do what He says He can do!"* I've included it below using the New Living Translation.

[18] As surely as God is faithful, our word to you does not waver between "Yes" and "No." [19] For Jesus Christ, the Son of God, does not waver between "Yes" and "No." He is the one whom Silas, Timothy, and I preached to you, and as God's ultimate "Yes," He always does what He says. [20] For all of God's promises have been fulfilled in Christ with a resounding "Yes!" And through Christ, our "Amen" (which means "Yes") ascends to God for His glory.

This passage continues to be significant in the transformation of my thinking. Let's consider how these verses challenge us.

1. Who is God's ultimate "Yes?" (verse 19) _____

Paul is making the point that Jesus Christ, about whom he had preached, is the "Yes" to all of God's promises found in scripture. And our response to this truth should be "Amen," which means "Yes." When we say yes to Christ's fulfillment of God's promises, the Holy Spirit imparts security to us as believers. As we move from thinking, "Maybe God can do that," to thinking "God can do what He says He can do," we cultivate a stronger belief in God. That produces faith that leads to living a life that glorifies God.

2. Share some of God's promises that are a clear "Yes" in your life.

3. Are there any ways you are limiting Him in your life?

When I was first confronted with "God can do what He says He can do," I began to realize just how much I had limited God in my life. I remember driving home from Bible study that day, with tears running down my cheeks as I wrangled with my exposed unbelief. While I could state lots of God's promises, my actions indicated that I didn't fully believe them. I desperately desired to have the confidence that Paul states in 2 Corinthians 1:20, and was ready to put in the work needed to change my thinking.

Knowing Paul's confidence in God's fulfillment of His promises is a great backdrop for Philippians 1:6.

4. Fill in the blanks. Paul, "being confident of this very thing, that _____ who has begun a _____ in you will _____ until the day of _____."

In the midst of his thankfulness, Paul finds joy in his anticipation of what God is going to do for the believers in the Philippian church. He has an absolute confidence, which goes far beyond human hope, because it is found on his knowledge and belief of God's fulfillment of His promises.

God's "good work" applies to the work of salvation and Christian living. Our works do not save us (Ephesians 2:8-9). Rather, salvation is God's work divinely initiated and divinely accomplished (Ephesians 2:4-8, Titus 3:4-6). This work will continue until we see Christ. Everything that God starts He will finish. Nothing will keep Him from the completion of what He has started (1 Thessalonians 5:24). The day of Christ Jesus refers to when believers will fully share the Lord's perfect righteousness (Galatians 4:19, Colossians 3:4).

New Testament scholar and Bible commentator William Hendriksen observed, "God…is not like men. Men conduct experiments, but God carries out a plan. God never does anything by halves." This really speaks to me because of my science background. God is not "messing around" with our lives. He is purposeful in everything that He does. Scientists experiment to see what will happen, but God already knows the result! As He carries out His plan for your life, there is no circumstance, person, or struggle that surprises Him. Paul knows that no matter what, one day we will be made perfect.

The more I have worked to build my confidence on the truth that God will do what He says He will do, I find myself saying, "God is not surprised by that." What is surprising to me is not surprising to God. I can trust Him to fulfill every promise, regardless of how bleak things look or how crazy things seem in my life. His plan is perfect for my life, and He completes what He starts! Lay claim to the confidence Paul had and make it your own! Christ will perfect you.

5. Where in your life do you feel "unfinished, lacking, or incomplete?"

6. How does your knowing that God will complete His work in you encourage you today with the circumstances, people, or struggles you are experiencing?

7. Has anything happened recently that surprises you? How does knowing that God is not surprised encourage you?

Journal today by completing this statement: "I most struggle to trust God to fulfill His promises because

_____

_____

_____

_____

_____

_____

_____

_____."

GOSPEL MINDSET
Day 4

READ PHILIPPIANS 1:1-11.

Paul tenderly loves the Philippian believers. They are his spiritual partners in furthering the Gospel. The word "affection" in verse eight actually refers to a person's bowels, which for the Hebrews included the heart, lungs, and liver. Often, the heart is associated with love, mercy, compassion, and kindness. Developing a Gospel Mindset requires thinking grounded in God's love. Let's look at Paul's prayer.

1. In verses 9-11, what does Paul specifically pray for concerning the love of the Philippian believers?

2. Use a dictionary to compare and contrast the meanings of knowledge and discernment.

Paul prays for abounding love. The word love here means "agape" or "brotherly love." It is a love that is genuine and decisive; a love that compels *us* to love, whether others are lovable or not, and whether they respond or not. It is the same version of love found in Romans 5:8: "But God demonstrates his own love for us in this: While we were still sinners, Christ died for us." John 13:34 records the Lord's command to "love one another, even as I have loved you," and when we obey that command we become "imitators of God, as beloved children" (Ephesians 5:1). In order to have an overflowing love for others, we need to connect to our only reliable knowledge source, the Bible! As we are obedient to the truth of God's word, we gain depth of insight into God's ways, which allows us to love God more fully and love others more genuinely.

3. Who in your life right now is difficult to love? Why?

4. What are the three results of abounding love that Paul prays for in verse 10?

Paul prays for discerning approval. Believers are to "approve the things that are excellent." This means to test, determine, and carefully identify whatever is the best, the most important, the most crucial. We must evaluate, daily, the thoughts on which we base our opinions and lifestyle. We need a single-minded focus on Christ that encourages our thinking to bring glory and honor to God. Our thoughts ultimately determine how we live, which furthers — or hinders — the Gospel.

Do you enjoy people-watching? Perhaps while you are sitting at the mall food court, observing all the interactions going on around you? I recently had some friends refer to people-watching as "people-judging." As soon as I heard that, I wanted to say, "No. That isn't it at all." But the Holy Spirit pricked my conscience. "They are right, Elizabeth. You are judging when you are watching." Ouch, right?

Ladies, if I am to love people with an abounding love, then I have to learn to put aside my personal preferences so that I can focus on God's interest in others. I cannot do that if my thinking focuses on judgment. Clearly, I must monitor my thoughts, to recognize when they aren't honoring God. When I have a judgmental thought about the way someone is dressed, or the singer who is off-key, I need to discern whether I should approve that thinking. Does it align with God's standards? If not, I must swiftly reject it and replace it with the truth of God's word. A Gospel Mindset means keeping our thoughts grounded in God's love for others. And who made me their judge, anyway?!

5. Where do you struggle most in judging others? Do you find your judgments are based on God's standards or human standards?

Paul also prays for sincerity and not taking offense. As used in this biblical text, the word sincere means "to judge by the sunlight," which was a method used in ancient days to uncover jar cracks that had been filled with wax by unscrupulous jar makers. This ancient practice provides a great metaphor we can use in our own life. We so often try to disguise our "cracks" with life choices we make about our clothing, hair color, accessories, church attendance, and spiritual talk. We might fool people, but God always knows our thoughts and intents (Hebrews 4:12). The phrase "without offense" means we should not fall into sinful behavior or cause others, whether saved or unsaved, to fall into sin. "Until the day of Christ" gives us the duration of our lifetime to actively pursue this goal.

Ladies I'm not proud to admit this, but I spent years of my life being insincere and completely unconcerned about whether I was potentially causing others to sin. I entered adulthood so focused on having it "all together" on the outside, that I had to hide my mess on the inside. I dressed well, spoke well, attended church, and could easily quote scripture. But it took a great deal of wax to fill in my cracks! My focus on making *me* look good, however, was not making Christ look attractive. The more I studied God's Word, the more He revealed those cracks! It was difficult. Some days I was ready to fight for right thinking, while other days, I just wanted to ignore it all. I look back now and praise God for His grace in my struggle. I praise God for the freedom of knowing that He is sufficient to fill my every crack.

> MY FOCUS ON MAKING ME LOOK GOOD, HOWEVER, WAS NOT MAKING CHRIST LOOK ATTRACTIVE.

Are there any cracks or areas of offense in your life that God is bringing to mind? Journal today about those cracks, including any excuses you've given God for not dealing with the cracks He has revealed to you.

GOSPEL MINDSET
Day 5

Yesterday we began looking at Paul's prayer. Let's refresh our memory. Read Philippians 1:1-11 again and fill in the blanks below.

That you may be filled _____ of _____,
which are _____ Jesus Christ, to the _____
of God.

Paul prays for the Philippians to be filled with the fruit of righteousness. The phrase "filled with" indicates to make full, to fill to the top. Another variation is to carry through to the end, to accomplish, to carry out. Once we are filled with the Holy Spirit, it works in us and through us to produce fruit for God. In Galatians 5:22-23, we read that the fruit of the Spirit is "love, joy, peace, patience, kindness, goodness, gentleness, faithfulness, and self-control." This fruit is possible because of the righteousness we receive through Jesus Christ!

1. Which fruit of the Spirit is most challenging for you to live out, and why?

2. In your own words, define "righteousness."

Righteousness is a word we hear often at church. But I think we miss the depth of meaning conveyed by it. Strong's Exhaustive Concordance of the Bible defines righteousness as "the state of him who is as he ought to be, righteousness, the condition acceptable to God."[2] We inherited our sinful nature. That sin makes us unacceptable before God, which makes us unacceptable to come into His presence. Romans 5:10 calls us "enemies with God."

But God provided a way for each of us to return to a "right standing." That way was Jesus' death on the cross. When we accept by faith Christ's finished work on the cross, He becomes our righteousness (1 Corinthians 1:30). We return to a condition acceptable to God! Glory, Halleluiah!

3. Knowing that Jesus became our righteousness, what thoughts should we dwell on about the cross?

The final phrase in Paul's prayer is "to the glory and praise of God." Every thought we entertain — *which leads to every action we take* — should glorify and praise God! The fruit we bear should proclaim the work that Jesus Christ is doing in us and through us. After all, Christ Himself lives within us! He empowers us with the Spirit to bear fruit. It is then that people see Jesus, rather than us.

> EVERY THOUGHT WE ENTERTAIN — *WHICH LEADS TO EVERY ACTION WE TAKE* — SHOULD GLORIFY AND PRAISE GOD!

4. What areas of your life do you tend to try to control, rather than allowing Christ to work in and through you?

Journal today about which verses from Philippians 1-11 you think can improve your thinking. Also write the verses on a notecard to carry with you. Commit to dwelling on the verses daily to cultivate a Gospel Mindset!

Week 2

NO MATTER WHAT MINDSET

LISTENING GUIDE
Philippians 1:12-30

NO MATTER WHAT...

I. God Uses Your Circumstances

    A. _____.

    B. _____.

II. Christ is Worth It

    A. Worth the _____.

    B. Worth the _____ of _____.

    C. Worth the _____.

III. Live to Further the Gospel

    A. _____.

    B. _____.

    C. _____.

No Matter What
MINDSET

NO MATTER WHAT MINDSET
Day 1

This week you'll study and think about the remainder of Philippians 1. Paul challenges us to focus on the cross and not our circumstances. Visit www. elizabethmahusay.com to access and watch the No Matter What Mindset video and fill in the listening guide.

READ PHILIPPIANS 1:1-14.

Paul now turns to address the specifics of his circumstances. He knows of the Philippians' concern for him, as they had sent Epaphroditus to inquire of Paul and to minister to him (Philippians 2:25). Verse 12, in which Paul says, "the things which happened to me have actually turned out for the furtherance of the Gospel," lays out the theme for these verses.

As we look to Paul's example, we can rightly consider him a pioneer of his day. Webster's dictionary defines pioneer as "-n. a person who goes before, preparing the way for others; -vt. to prepare or open." That is what Paul did in his obedience to preach in Philippi. He advanced the Gospel in that Roman colony. Now, from his Roman prison cell, Paul reflects on how "the things which happened" have been tools that furthered or "pioneered" the Gospel.

1. Has someone in your life gone before you, preparing the way for you to be responsive to the Gospel? What is one specific action this person did?

2. What two groups were impacted by Paul's chains (verses 13-14)? How so?

Paul refers to his chains or imprisonment many times in these verses, making it clear that his circumstances are dire. Yet because he is single-minded in his desire to see the Gospel preached, he does not complain about his chains or take a break from sharing the Gospel. Paul sees opportunity in the obstacle. He declares, "My chains are in Christ." The entire palace guard becomes aware of the Gospel, as a guard is chained to Paul in shifts, all day, every day.

What a great perspective Paul has about his circumstances. God uses Paul's chains to advance the Gospel and encourage other believers in Christ to be confident in their own circumstances. The result is their having "far more courage to speak the word of God without fear" (verse 14).

> *"Sometimes God has to put 'chains' on His people to get them to accomplish a 'pioneer advance' that could never happen any other way."*
> —*Warren Wiersbe*

The fact that Paul is chained and unable to travel gives him ample time to read, study, reflect, and listen to the Lord. As a result, we benefit from his Prison Epistles: Ephesians, Colossians, Philippians, and Philemon—four of the 13 New Testament books traditionally attributed to Paul.

3. How much time do you spend reading the Bible, praying, and telling others about the Lord? Would you describe yourself as committed like Paul, or is your life so "busy" that they get placed on the back burner?

4. List some "chains" you feel you have in your life that hinder you and your service to God.

It can be hard to confess what we really feel are "chains." After all, if we admit that we feel the care of our children often feels more like "chains" than joyful mothering, what will people think? I can remember when my boys were toddlers and everything seemed like a chore. I was angry a lot. I can remember feeling resentful that I had to give up singing in choir so our boys were not constantly in church daycare. Yet, that period of my life was the beginning of God making room in my life for His better plan. Room for attending women's Bible studies, which led to facilitating studies, which led to writing and teaching studies. Praise God for the chains!

5. Share how God has used your "chains" to accomplish His best for your life.

Journal today by recording what comes to mind when you consider that God can use even your "chains" to further His Gospel!

NO MATTER WHAT MINDSET
Day 2

READ PHILIPPIANS 1:1-18.

1. List the two groups preaching, along with their motives.

Both groups Paul references in verses 15-18 are preaching about Christ. While their content is the same (the redemption Christ provides), their motives are completely different. Those preaching out of envy (jealousy) and strife (contention) desire to discredit Paul, promote themselves, and aggravate and intensify Paul's distress over the condition of the church. Those preaching "from good will" have positive motives, which include their love, appreciation, and support for Paul's work.

2. What is Paul's response to these two groups?

Paul's response of rejoicing is a result of a transformed Mindset that God developed in him. Responding positively to a clearly negative situation is not natural. Rather, it is a *supernatural* response made possible by the work of the Holy Spirit in our thinking. To understand this better, let's compare a negative and a positive thought response to these ill-motive teachers. *The Power of Thought* graphic, located in Appendix A, illustrates how our thoughts lead to actions. Place yourself in Paul's shoes as you move through the following exercise.

Starting Negative Thought: <u>Who do these people think they are in trying to discredit me?</u>

Belief: _____

Expectation: _____

Attitude: _____

Action: _____

Starting Positive Thought: <u>God is not surprised that these people are trying to discredit me.</u>

Belief: _____

Expectation: _____

Attitude: _____

Action: _____

What attitude and action develop from negative thinking? Clearly, starting with a positive Mindset produces a very different result. A positive result! As Paul looks at the big picture, he sees Christ proclaimed — regardless of the motives of those preaching. He recognizes that God could use a positive mindset.

Let's do this exercise again, using a situation in your life. Recall a recent negative circumstance in which you had a negative thought response. Anything instantly spring to mind — and spear you in the heart? Definitely list it below!

The circumstance: _____

Starting Negative Thought: _____

Belief: _____

Expectation: _____

Attitude: _____

Action: _____

Now turn it around and work through the process again, but this time from a positive thought response.

Starting Positive Thought: _____

Belief: _____

Expectation: _____

Attitude: _____

Action: _____

Journal today any fresh insights you received from the Lord as you worked through the *Power of Thought* process. Are there circumstances in your life that trigger a negative thought response? Did God bring to mind the need to reconcile with anyone?

NO MATTER WHAT MINDSET
Day 3

READ PHILIPPIANS 1:1-20.

1. By what means does Paul expect to be delivered (vs. 19)? Check two.
   - ❏ His own strength
   - ❏ The government
   - ❏ Prayers of the saints
   - ❏ His lawyer
   - ❏ The Spirit of Christ

Paul expresses his expectation of deliverance. The King James version reads "salvation," which means "preservation or safety." In some New Testament uses, salvation indicates spiritual deliverance. Let's look at a wonderful treasure I discovered as I was studying this word using one of my favorite online resources, BlueletterBible.org:

> *Sōtēria: future salvation, the sum of benefits and blessings, which the Christians, redeemed from all earthly ills, will enjoy after the visible return of Christ from heaven in the consummated and eternal kingdom of God.*

When Paul says, "For I know that this will turn out for my deliverance," he makes it clear that no matter what, he will enjoy the benefits and blessings of eternity with God. He knows the Philippian believers are praying for him, and he expects the support of the Spirit of Jesus Christ.

2. Name someone who is praying for you, and share how that encourages you.

Paul's earnest desire is the magnification of Christ. "As always, so now also Christ will be magnified in my body." Just as a telescope magnifies the stars to bring them closer, or a microscope that makes tiny things look bigger, our body is the lens through which unbelievers see Christ. Though Paul is not sure whether he will be released from prison or face a martyr's death, his Mindset was to courageously face death with a positive attitude. Paul's hope is that his testimony magnifies his Lord.

When my best friend, Heather, was in the last days of her battle with breast cancer, I made the 10-hour trip to see her for the last time. I was amazed at how, within just 24 hours, she went from lucid, to snatches of consciousness, to a coma-like sleep. Heather displayed such faith in her fight; she expected God's deliverance. She approached death with an amazing attitude and died with grace and dignity. Heather's attitude had a profound influence on her friend, Jennifer. The very next day Jennifer accepted Christ! Heather's body was the lens by which God magnified Christ for Jennifer, and it changed her eternity!

3. What have you learned about dealing with challenging circumstances from these verses?

4. What makes it hard for you to face difficult circumstances with courage and a Paul-like attitude?

Journal today with statements describing the testimony you want to leave for Christ when your journey ends.

NO MATTER WHAT MINDSET
Day 4

READ PHILIPPIANS 1:1-26.

   1. Looking at verses 21-26, what is good about dying and living?

As he writes this letter, Paul is "hard-pressed" between life and death. He knows that by living he will be able to continue working at "the salvation of sinners, the edification of saints, the establishment of churches, the training of new leaders, and the writing of inspired Scripture," as Bible commentator Robert Gromacki puts it.[3] Paul also knows that the moment of his death will bring departure from his earthly life, to an eternity spent in the presence of his single-minded focus, Christ Jesus. No wonder he feels "hard-pressed between the two."

   2. What is the press for you to keep living?

   3. In your own words, what does death mean for you?

Paul's struggle between life and death highlights the "no matter what" mindedness he has toward the growth of the Philippian believers. Even though he knows death will be "far better," he is willing to continue to deal with the hardships of life and ministry for the benefit of his friends.

   4. As you focus on verse 25, underline the two things Paul expects to accomplish within the Philippian believers through living: "And

being confident of this, I know that I shall remain and continue with you all for your progress and joy of faith."

Paul states that he expects to return to Philippi, and that their rejoicing will be abundant and overflowing in Jesus Christ. After all, the return of the man who originally taught them about Jesus Christ would certainly be reason to celebrate.

5. Who first introduced you to Jesus Christ? What three things could you say to this person, that would speak to the depth of your relationship with Christ?

Journal today with the names of those you want to introduce to Jesus Christ during your lifetime. List ways that you might begin that introduction with the person(s) the Holy Spirit brings to mind. Or, share how God used you to lead someone to Christ. How did that feel?

NO MATTER WHAT MINDSET
Day 5

READ PHILIPPIANS 1:1-30.

Focusing on verses 27 and 28, list out what Paul hopes to hear about the Philippian brothers and sisters in Christ.

1. _____

2. With one mind _____

3. _____

In verse 27 Paul addresses the "conduct" or behavior of the Philippian believers. He admonishes them to live "worthy of the Gospel of Christ," so that "you stand fast in one spirit, with one mind striving together for the faith of the Gospel." The phrase "the faith of the Gospel" refers to the body of truth divinely inspired and given to the church. Paul also encourages them to not be terrified by their adversaries. Let's look at each of these phrases to learn more.

SATAN IS WAGING A WAR TO STEAL THE VERY BELIEFS AND DOCTRINES THAT ARE DISTINCTIVELY CHRISTIAN.

Standing Together: We are in a battle for our Christian faith. Satan is waging a war to steal the very beliefs and doctrines that are distinctively Christian. His approach is often subtle. Oswald Chambers calls it a temptation to "shift our view."

1. What are some common messages that TV, radio, books, and social media bombard Christians with in order to promote a "shift in view?"

Popular statements like "To each his own," "God is the same in every religion, He just goes by a different name," and "Everyone deserves to be happy" are examples of how "the faith of the Gospel" has been eroded in the minds of many believers. The tragedy is that when we think such lies are true, we develop wrong beliefs about God and man's expected response to God's truth. These wrong beliefs lead to wrong attitudes and behavior. Before long, believers sound and act like the world.

I can remember being in college and not walking with the Lord. I had stopped reading my Bible, was not attending church, and I only prayed when I needed a parachute to soften the blow of falling hard from bad choices! As a result, the world heavily influenced me. In that season of my life, I went from being completely pro-life to justifying pro-choice. While I did not believe I would choose abortion for myself, I was not applying the truth that God counts all life as precious, even life in the womb. I praise God for His grace and that He kept pursuing me to return to the truth hidden in my heart. Getting back into church, reading my Bible, and praying more consistently was significant in God transforming my thoughts on key truths, such as the sanctity of life.

> 2. As you walk with Christ, which of the world's lies has been the hardest for you to reject? Share why.

We must stand together as the Church and fight against the world's lies using the spiritual weapons God provides, namely His Word and prayer (Hebrews 4:12; Ephesians 6:11-18). God's Word gives us "one mind" as we strive together. It provides the cohesion we need to stand side-by-side and fight our enemy. We must depend on the Holy Spirit to give us that power.

If we are to strive together, we must cultivate a "one mind" approach to living. Just as an athletic team must work together to achieve victory, so must we stand together in Christ to defeat Satan. Games are not won on the sidelines or by trying to coach from the bleachers. In the same way that a player can't expect one weekly practice session to prepare him or her for the game, we can't expect that attending church once a week will be enough to prepare us for the fight. We need to be in the Word daily, allowing God to transform our thinking.

3. The table below is part of *One-to-One Discipling*, a 9-lesson study created by Multiplication Ministries.[4] It is designed to be used by one person to disciple another person to have a strong, foundational faith. Use the table to analyze your habits for being in the Word. As you fill in the table, pray about setting new goals.

Intake of the Word	My Present Weekly Program	New Goals & Plans
Hearing i.e. Sunday Sermon.		
Reading i.e. YouVersion Bible Plan.		
Studying i.e. Quiet Time, A Bible Study like this one.		
Memorizing i.e. Specific scriptures you are committing to memory.		
Meditating i.e. Biblical truths you are pondering.		

As we stand together and strive together, we can expect opposition. But God exhorts us to not be afraid.

Philippians 1:28 encourages readers to not be "terrified by your adversaries," because it shows two things: that 1) Opponents of the Gospel are destined for an eternity of hell, and 2) It gives evidence of our salvation. (See 2 Thessalonians 1:4-8).

The word "perdition" is translated as "destroying, utter destruction." Compare that to the translation of salvation, which is "deliverance, preservation, and safety." Paul uses the same Greek root word for salvation here that he used in verse 19. In the same way that Paul is certain of his deliverance, he is certain of the Philippian believer's deliverance!

4. How does knowing that God promises deliverance to you strengthen you for the daily fight for right thinking?

5. What two things does Paul say, in verse 29, are granted on behalf of Christ to the Philippian believers?

On behalf of Christ, both belief and suffering are gifts that God grants to His children. We all like to open the gift of salvation, but few of us see suffering as a gift. Am I right, ladies? Yet Jesus, in Matthew 5:10-12, calls those who suffer "blessed."

In Matthew 10:22 Jesus says, "You will be hated by all because of My name, but it is the one who has endured to the end who will be saved." In Matthew 11:29-30 He commands, "Take my yoke upon you and learn from me, for I am gentle and humble in heart, and you will find rest for your souls. For my yoke is easy and my burden is light." Suffering for Christ is a privilege. Paul assures us, in verse 30, that we are not alone in our suffering. We must look at suffering in the light of Jesus Christ and our heavenly inheritance (1 Peter 1:6-8). When we suffer for Christ's sake, our faith is tested and proved genuine. But, as it says in 1 Peter 2:19-20, when our sin results in suffering, our suffering is of no credit.

6. Are you suffering for Christ in some area of your life? Are your beliefs being ridiculed at work, for example?

7. What part of today's study has most encouraged you in your thinking on suffering?

Journal today by recording truths you gathered from I Peter 1:6-8. Meditate on these truths to cultivate a No Matter What Mindset about suffering.

Week 3

CHRIST-LIKE
EVERYDAY MINDSET

LISTENING GUIDE
Philippians 2

In order for Christ to increase:

I must: _____.

I must: _____.

I must: _____.

I must: _____.

Cultivate a Christ-like Everyday Mindset by:

I. Humble Interactions

    A. Promote _____.

    B. Promote _____.

II. Humble Obedience

    A. Requires _____.

    B. Requires _____.

    C. Requires _____.

III. Humble Emulation

Christ-Like Everyday
MINDSET

CHRIST-LIKE EVERYDAY MINDSET
Day 1

This week you'll study all of Philippians 2 which challenges you to humbly decrease so that Christ can increase. Visit www.elizabethmahusay.com to access and watch the Christ-like Everyday Mindset video and fill in the listening guide.

READ PHILIPPIANS 2.

Paul shares his Gospel Mindset in Philippians 1. When we have a desire to further the Gospel, we can cultivate a "no matter what" perspective of our circumstances. In this chapter he looks at what Christ-like Everyday Mindset entails: a humble, submissive mind. The dictionary defines submissive as "having or showing a tendency to submit without resistance; yielding." In simpler terms, we are yielding to the action, control, or power of another or others.

Paul tells his Philippian brothers and sisters that this yielding is to be given to other like-minded individuals. He speaks to this in Ephesians 5:21 when he says, "Submit to one another out of reverence for Christ." (NIV) Yet culture tells us that submission is a sign of weakness. It bombards us with messaging that we need to be self-sufficient and independent. To look out for number one. To even expect others to take advantage of us, if we let our guard down. We adopt lines of thinking such as, "What if I submit and I am cheated out of what is rightly mine?" Thoughts like this can lead us to develop a "me" mentality, which makes it difficult for us to lay aside our personal preferences and opinions. But God calls us to trust Him and humbly submit to the truth of His Word when interacting with others. In short, we are to choose to be Christ-like every day, regardless of the actions of others.

Let's look at why Paul decides to teach this Mindset. He is facing problems with teachers in Rome (Philippians 1:15-18), as well as the believers of Philippi (Philippians 4:2). Epaphroditus, a Philippian church messenger who ministered to Paul's needs, brought news of a church division centering on Euodia and Syntyche. While we're not told the specifics of the division, it is clear that Paul feels it imperative to teach about the issue of unity within the church. Unity is the outgrowth of individuals who, in humility, are willing to be "Christ-like Everyday" as they serve and sacrifice.

Paul begins chapter 2 with "Therefore," which refers back to verse 1:27, in which Paul admonishes the Philippians to strive together with one mind.

To conduct ourselves worthy of the Gospel of Christ, with one spirit and one mind, we must fulfill Paul's four conditional "ifs" listed in verse one. Do you remember learning about If/Then statements in school? An If/Then statement stipulates that in order to achieve our desired result, we must meet the condition of the "if." For example: If I study for the test, then I can expect a better grade. Let's look at how Paul uses the If/Then construct in verses 1 and 2.

1. List the four "if" statements that describe the right motives of spiritual unity.

2. What is the "then" that Paul gives in verse 2? "Fulfill my joy by…"

Let's combine these If/Then statements to learn practical ways to cultivate unity through Christ:

If there is any consolation/encouragement in Christ, then be like-minded. Encouragement has the root meaning of "coming alongside someone to give assistance by offering comfort, counsel, or warning." This is the role of the Holy Spirit in our lives. In John 14:16 Jesus prays for "another helper, that He may abide with you forever." As we yield to the Spirit's help, we each are able to develop the like-mindedness that is needed within the church. My challenge is yielding. I must continually submit my wants and desires to the Holy Spirit's direction.

If there is any comfort of love, then have that same love toward one another. God demonstrates this comfort of love by sending Christ to die while we were still sinners (Romans 5:8). God loves us enough to make relationship with Him possible. We could say that He loves us even when we are unlovable. The depth and genuineness of His love should compel us to demonstrate this same love to others.

If we are to have any fellowship of the Spirit, then we must be of one accord or united in spirit. Fellowship, as we discussed in Chapter 1, describes partnership and mutual sharing. This fellowship should produce a desire to be united which means "one-souled." It means to live in selfless harmony with fellow believers and, by definition, excludes personal ambition, selfishness, hatred, envy, jealousy, and the countless other evils that are the fruits of self-love.

If there is any affection and mercy/compassion, then be of one mind. Our job is to yield to the Holy Spirit for the cultivation of like-mindedness. The Holy Spirit then produces care and concern for other believers within us.

3. Check which of the four if/then statements you struggle with the most and share why.

   ❏ Yielding to the comfort, counsel, or warning of the Holy Spirit.
   ❏ Loving people when they are unlovable.
   ❏ Living selflessly with other believers.
   ❏ Extending mercy to others even when you don't feel like it.

I struggle the most with extending mercy to others. I can be quick to judge if I am not walking in the Spirit. My challenge with judging is that I usually judge others in areas where I believe I tend to do well or do not necessarily struggle. I have to constantly remind myself that I, too, am a work in progress!

In verse 2, Paul asks the Philippians to "fulfill" his joy. Using an If/Then statement, we could rewrite that as "If you do these things as a church, then you will make my joy complete."

Choosing one mind, one love, and one spirit cultivates a humble, submissive mind. True joy can grow out of a submissive mind. Ladies, the acronym of **J**esus first, **O**thers next, and **Y**ourself last can become our way of life!

4. Verses 3 and 4 list five action steps to achieving spiritual unity. Record them below. Then circle three things from the list to avoid.

5. In what areas of your life do you tend to display selfish ambition or conceit? Conceit means "an excessively favorable opinion of one's own ability, importance, wit, etc."

When I was in college, my selfish ambition and conceit centered primarily on how great I thought I was as a student. If I wanted to make an A, I would study endless hours in preparation. I took pride in the fact that I would go to bed at 7pm, to get up at 2am to study six hours before my final Physics exam. Crazy, right?!

Once I got married, my selfish ambition showed up in my agenda always taking priority over my husband's agenda. While I never said aloud that my goals were more important than his, I certainly behaved in a way that revealed my thinking. I can look back now and honestly admit that I was so disrespectful. I often treated Fred as though he were my child, rather than honoring him as my husband.

6. Verse 4 commands us to look out for the interests of others. What are some practical ways you can selflessly look out for the interests of others?

Your spouse:

Your children:

Your neighbors:

Your friends:

The person that is stomping on your last nerve:

Journal today by listing at least one area of your life in which you struggle with selfish ambition or conceit. Think about ways you can lessen this struggle. Write out a prayer to God specific to this struggle.

CHRIST-LIKE EVERYDAY MINDSET
Day 2

READ PHILIPPIANS 2:1-11.

Yesterday we looked at the need for cultivating a humble, submissive attitude. As we continue reading in chapter 2, Paul reminds us that our thinking cultivates attitudes that we express through our behavior. Today let's consider four distinct patterns of thought or Mindsets that I believe are demonstrated through Christ's attitude and actions. If we are to live as Christ every day, then we need to anchor our thinking in Christ's example.

The first pattern Jesus has is an "I will be second" Mindset (verse 6).

1. Jot down how the following verses also describe Jesus.

Verse	Describe who Jesus is...
John 1:1-2, 14	
Colossians 1:15	
Hebrews 1:2-3	

Jesus does not stop being God when He comes to earth. He is still just as holy, all-powerful, all- knowing, and sovereign as the Father. Yet, He "did not regard equality with God a thing to be grasped." (Philippians 2:6). Christ willingly sets aside His divine rights and privileges to become a man and serve others. He becomes second to put the needs of humanity first.

The second pattern Jesus Christ has is "I will be a servant" Mindset (verse 7).

The word bondservant in this verse is doulas, which means "slave or bondman." Jesus yields His will to that of His Father's will so that He can serve by "emptying Himself." Jesus does not think less of Himself; He made the choice to think of others before Himself. His time spent alone and in prayer always leads Him back to the priority of serving others.

2. What is God's attitude toward Jesus as He does this? (Matthew 3:17). What is God's attitude toward us when we give up our rights and surrender our will to His ways? (Matthew 25:21, 23).

3. What rights do you feel God is calling you to surrender today?

The third pattern Jesus Christ has is an "I will sacrifice" Mindset (verse 8).

Jesus willingly sacrifices His place at the side of the Father to become fully human. He is able to humble Himself because He knows that He will return to the Father. Jesus sacrifices His life, becoming "obedient unto death, even the death of the cross" because the end goal of His earthly life is His willing sacrifice of Himself for the sins of the world. It is important to note that Jesus suffers a real death, enduring all the agony that comes with it.

4. Use a dictionary to look up the meaning of the word "sacrificial." Write down the definition.

5. What area of your life most challenges you to sacrifice yourself? What has helped or hindered you from having a sacrificial mentality in obedience to God's Word?

The fourth pattern Jesus has is an "I will humble Myself" Mindset. (verses 8-11).

Christ chose to humble Himself to serve others and carry the unimaginable burden of the world's sin. Because of His obedience, God "exalted Him" above anyone or anything. This exalting involves the bestowing "on Him the name which is above every name" (verse 9).

6. Using verse 11, fill in the blank. Jesus Christ is _____.

The word "Lord" is the title of majesty, authority, honor, and sovereignty. God gives Jesus the name to fulfill the prophesy that "every knee shall bow" and "every tongue shall take an oath" that Jesus is Lord (Isaiah 45:22-23).

7. All people, angels, and demons will worship Jesus on that day. Match the groups given on the left with their location on the right. (verse 10).

Redeemed Believers of All Ages and Angels	Those on the Earth
Redeemed and Unredeemed Still Living	Those Under the Earth
Dead Unredeemed People and Fallen Angels	Those in Heaven

8. All people will call Him "Lord," but not all people will call Him "Savior." According to Romans 10:9-10, 13, who can call Jesus "Savior"?

9. Can you call Him "Savior"? If someone were to ask you how you came to accept Jesus, how would you respond? Write out your three- to five-sentence testimony below.

I remember, at the age of seven, attending a special service at the church my family attended. I realized that night that I wanted what my parents had — a personal relationship with Jesus. I walked to the front of the church and shared my desire with the staff. That was the night I knew Jesus had saved me. I have called Him Savior ever since.

> HE WAS NOT LORD OF MY LIFE.

I would love to tell you that I went on to live with a consistent Christ-like Mindset after that, but I didn't. Some years I pursued God hard; some years I kept God on my shelf. In my early thirties I was confronted with the reality that I believed God for my salvation, but *He was not Lord of my life*. I needed to cultivate a Christ-like Mindset.

10. Which of these is the hardest for you? Record why.

   ❏ "I will be second" Mindset.
   ❏ "I will be a servant" Mindset.
   ❏ "I will sacrifice" Mindset.
   ❏ "I will be humble" Mindset.

My primary love language is acts of service; I really enjoy finding ways I can be a servant. My challenge is addressing my motive for doing the serving. Rather than glorifying God, my motive can easily move from simply serving to being *recognized* for my serving or sacrificing. And sometimes I am guilty of serving to get something in return. At times I have served to benefit my needs and the use of my time. Just writing that admission is hard for me, but I have learned that motives matter. God searches my heart and He knows my motives.

Two passages of scripture that I have prayed often are Psalm 139:23-24 and Philippians 2:3-4. Look up both passages and journal about what speaks to you. Write a prayer to God regarding your desire to have a Christ-like Mindset. As you pray, be still and listen.

CHRIST-LIKE EVERYDAY MINDSET
Day 3

READ PHILIPPIANS 2:1-15.

Today we focus our attention on verses 12-15. "Therefore, my beloved," in verse 12 refers to Christ's example of humble submission to the will of God in order to accomplish God's plan (verses 5-11). The Philippian Christians, Paul's beloved, need to follow Paul's instruction, which he draws from Christ's example. To live successful "Christ-like Everyday" lives, we, too, need to follow Paul's instructions.

When my two boys were young, I specifically remember explaining to them why my husband and I wanted them to behave in certain ways. Our goal was to invest in their moral warehouse, so that when we were not around to ensure compliance, they would choose to do the right thing on their own. It took so much more time to tell them why instead of just saying, "Don't do that!" The command to "Don't" would have provided short-term compliance, but done very little to prepare them for self-governance.

Rather than telling the Philippians what **not** to do, Paul commands them what to do.

1. Record Paul's command from verse 12.

The phrase "work out" does not refer to a works-based salvation. The Philippian believers were already saved. This phrase carries the meaning of "work to full completion," or as Bible commentator Warren Weirsbe offers, "working a mine." Our "work" should complete the salvation that God has so graciously given us.[5] (See Ephesians 2:8-10.) When you work a mine, you are working to extract all the valuable ore that it contains. You know the ore is present, but you must appropriate or take possession of it. This may mean hammering away at the rock that hides the ore, or filtering out the unusable material in order to reveal what is of value. I like to use the word "appropriate" because it reminds me that I am an active participant in God's plan, and I must take hold of that which God has provided for me. We must each *take possession* of the valuable resources that God has given us, and proactively pursue our purpose.

2. List what you are presently doing to "appropriate" the valuable resources God has given you.

3. Write the promise given in verse 13.

God gives us the Holy Spirit to energize us for the task of "working out our salvation." It is an in/out process. What God works *in us*, we are to work *out* for the ultimate goal of achieving "Christlikeness." We cannot make progress in our "Christlikeness" if we do not allow God to work *in* us first. Verse 13 makes that clear. As Paul states in Philippians 1:27, we must "conduct ourselves worthy of the gospel of Christ." For God to work *through you,* He first works *in you* the character that He requires you to *work out* to learn to conduct yourself worthy. For example, God had Moses tend to sheep for 40 years before He commissioned him to go back to Egypt! God was working *in* and Moses was working *out*. We, too, need to work out what God is working in so He can transform our thinking.

4. Pause and consider what God is working *in* you during this season of your life. On the left, list the circumstance that God is using. On the right, jot down what you are working *out* because of the circumstance. I will use one of mine as an example.

Circumstance	What I Am Working Out
Ex. Paying down debt.	Stewardship, dependence on God, manna for today

I am so thankful for how God has been working *in* me as our family works to pay down debt. We have debt because of poor financial decisions, but God is faithful to "work all things together for good for those who love Him and are called according to His purpose" (Romans 8:28). Even though we are living in the consequences of our past choices, God is working in our present to prepare us for the certain future He knows is coming!

5. How are we to work out our salvation? (verse 14)

6. What should working in this manner produce? (verse 15)

7. How will Christ-followers appear to the watching world if they are obedient to the command found in verse 14?

Paul draws attention to that world in verses 14 and 15, when he contrasts the life of the believer with the lives of those who do not believe. Unsaved people complain and dispute because they have no hope of a heavenly home. But as Christians, we can rejoice! Secular society is "crooked and perverse" (verse 15), but as Christians we are able to live steadfastly, if we walk according to the perfect standard of God's Word. Unsaved people walk in darkness, groping for something to guide their way. As Christians, we have the Bible to lead us in our daily living (Psalm 119:105). As a result, we shine as bright lights to the world. The Holy Spirit works *in* us that we might live the "Christian-lit" life.

Journal today by listing what most often has you complaining or disputing. Then work backward to identify and list the thoughts that are foundational to your behavior.

CHRIST-LIKE EVERYDAY MINDSET
Day 4

READ PHILIPPIANS 2:1-18.

As we closed Day 3, I asked you to jot down the areas of your life that cause you to habitually dispute or complain. I did so to help you discover where you might be dimming your testimony as a follower of Christ. Why is it critical that you not dim your light? When we each live as a "light in the world," our unified light as the Church shines more brightly to a lost and dying world.

Picture yourself holding a lit candle in your hand. As you approach another person holding an unlit candle, you offer to light their candle with yours. This person can accept or refuse your offer, right? With this scene in mind, let's complete the following word study.

Look at the phrase in verse 16: "holding fast the word of life." Holding fast means to "hold toward, hold forth, to present." The Greek root for "word" is logos. John 1 uses the same root word.

1. Write out John 1:1 and 1:14.

2. "Word" refers to who in these two verses?

3. How might you restate the first part of Philippians 2:16, now that you know the meaning of these words?

Paul, in effect, asks the Philippian believers to hold out the message of Christ to others. Jesus, in the Sermon on the Mount, calls believers "the light of the world" and gives specific instructions for what we should do with our light.

4. Write out Matthew 5:16.

5. How are you allowing your "light to shine before men?"

6. Look again at Philippians 2:16. Why does Paul want the church of Philippi to "hold fast the word of life?"

Notice that Paul does not make his rejoicing contingent upon how others respond to the Philippian believers holding out the message of Christ. Rather, Paul's delight comes from knowing that their daily commitment to radiate Christ ensures they will live with a "Christ-like Everyday" Mindset.

7. What attitude does Paul maintain as his life is poured out for the sake of other believers? (Verse 17, 18)

Paul is willing that his life be "offered up" on the sacrifice and service of the Philippian believers' faith. The Greek root word for sacrifice is *thysia*. The same root word is found in Romans 12:1.

8. In Romans 12:1, what kind of sacrifice does Paul encourage believers to be?

Paul uses the image of the "pouring out as a drink offering" because it is a familiar metaphor of his time (Numbers 15:1-10 and Leviticus 23:18). Paul sees his life as the ultimate act of sacrifice to the Lord. In Romans 12:1 he writes, "…present your bodies a living sacrifice, holy, acceptable to God." In 2 Timothy 4:6 he adds, "For I am already being poured out as a drink offering, and the time of my departure is at hand."

This wording demonstrates Paul's willingness to sacrifice, even to the point of death. Paul's selfless, sacrificial service has caused him great suffering, but more importantly has brought him great joy (2 Corinthians 7:4; Colossians 1:24). Paul uses his own example to encourage the Philippian believers, with whom he has the mutual purpose of proclaiming Christ. Paul recognizes their faithfulness and desires to rejoice with them, and urges them to rejoice as well.

Do you remember the song *This Little Light of Mine*? I loved singing that song as a child. It was a great way to teach the basics of "Christ-like Everyday" living. We are to let our light shine every day and not hide it under a bushel.

For me, the "bushel" is most often my own self-sufficiency and independence. Ladies, when I start operating on my own strength, my "Christ-like" light becomes the "look-at-me" light. Yuck! The "look-at-me" light is dim and inadequate as a light for others living in a dark world.

Rather than filling people with hope and confidence of ongoing God empowerment, the "look-at-me" light causes others to compare their ability to mine. (I know this is true, because I often catch myself comparing myself to others!) When others look at me and decide they lack my apparent confidence, they might doubt their own abilities. If, on the other hand, they conclude they are like me or better than me, I have just pointed them to self-sufficiency rather than dependence on God! *Lord, help me to get out of Your way!*

> LORD, HELP ME TO GET OUT OF YOUR WAY!

READ MATTHEW 5:14-16.

Journal today by identifying the "bushels" that you sometimes use to hide Christ's light, whether knowingly or unknowingly. Pick one specific memory that comes to mind. How did you intentionally choose not to shine for Christ? What prompted your thoughts or action? What was the outcome on your testimony for Christ? If you could relive that moment, would you do things differently?

CHRIST-LIKE EVERYDAY MINDSET
Day 5

READ PHILIPPIANS 2:1-30.

Paul now turns his attention to the commendation of two wonderful examples, Timothy and Epaphroditus. These two men are of great help in Paul's ministry, and serve as examples of submissive-minded Christians. These two "ordinary saints" show us that service and sacrifice for the cause of Christ is both doable and rewarding. Our willingness to serve and sacrifice may not happen automatically, but our attitudes we can develop and cultivate as we walk with the Lord and allow Him to transform our thinking.

1. Use verses 20 and 21 to name Timothy's qualities that make him the perfect person to encourage the Philippian Church.

2. According to verse 22, how does Paul describe his relationship with Timothy?

3. Is anyone mentoring you today in the manner Paul mentors Timothy? Are you mentoring anyone? Briefly, describe these relationships.

Paul's imprisonment makes it impossible for him to visit the Philippian church, though he hopes to do so. But he is able to send Timothy to check on its health. Paul cares deeply for the spiritual growth of the Philippian church, as does Timothy. Paul refers to Timothy as "like-minded," which can be translated as "equal in soul."

The question that keeps coming to my mind is whether I care deeply about my church. Can my Pastor call me "like-minded" or "equal in soul?" I want to say yes, but I know that I am often seeking after my own interests. For example, focusing on accomplishing my "to do" list at the expense of what my church needs done in order to be missional in the community. I daily have to ask God to be Lord of my day. I have to allow for margin in my schedule so that I can respond to the appointments He has for me. I have learned to view this time as divine appointments rather than interruptions. I need to say, "I get to," rather than "I have to." As God gifts me with every moment of my day, I should live each moment for His honor and glory. Ladies, how we think about our time really does determine our attitude about our time. *Is your time your time — or God's time? Are you willing to be used by Him, even on the days you'd rather stick to your own agenda?*

> IS YOUR TIME YOUR TIME —
> OR GOD'S TIME?

4. Might your pastor call you "like-minded?" Share why or why not.

Let's look again at Epaphroditus, who truly demonstrates a submissive spirit. A member of the Philippian church, Epaphroditus travels to Rome to give Paul the church's missionary offering (verse 4:18). It is likely that the church intends him to stay and assist Paul indefinitely.

5. What are the three titles that Paul gives to Epaphroditus (verse 25)?

6. What is the reason for Epaphroditus' concern (verse 26)?

7. According to verse 27, upon whom does God have mercy?

Epaphroditus immediately begins to serve Paul upon his arrival. He is loyal, faithful, and wants to see the job to completion. Do you and I share the same commitment to serve? Bible commentator Warren Weirsbe remarked that the modern Church is in desperate need of men and women who feel burdened for missions.[6] In short, there are many spectators but not enough participants. Our single-minded focus on Christ should compel us to give and go into the world to proclaim salvation through faith in Jesus. A good gauge of the spiritual maturity of a church could be the amount of its outreach mission work. A good gauge of your own spiritual maturity is your own outreach mission work — whether in your neighborhood or in another country.

8. How are you giving and going to proclaim the Gospel?

When my husband and I moved from Florida to Texas, it took us a lot of time to emotionally and mentally work through leaving behind our friends, our strong business connections, and our growing church ministries. We felt alone, isolated, and fearful as the reality of having no friends, family, business connections, or ministry in our new city slammed into us.

Our missionary friends encouraged us to see ourselves as missionaries to the area and to commit our lives to the work of God. That encouragement made the difference for us as we set out to build relationships and serve those that God brought into our path. We did end up making friends, building new business connections, and finding ways to serve our community and our church. I tell people that moving across the country was both the best thing and the hardest thing we have ever done. But I am thankful for all that we have learned as a result. Perhaps you have experienced a similar move in your own life.

9. Most of us will not have to risk our lives for the sake of the Gospel. But serving Christ does cost us. What have you "left behind" for the work of Christ? To what are you still firmly holding?

Journal today with the thoughts that you want to anchor in your mind to develop a "Christ-like Everyday" Mindset.

Week 4

HEAVEN-FOCUSED MINDSET

LISTENING GUIDE
Philippians 3

HEAVEN-FOCUSED MINDSET PROVIDES PERSPECTIVE.

I. Perspective for Present Circumstances

    A. Are _____.

    B. Are _____.

    C. Are _____.

    D. Are _____.

II. Perspective for Past Credentials

   A. Often become _____.

   B. Give us a _____.

   C. Keep us in _____.

III. Perspective for Purposed Counting

   A. Requires knowing _____.

   B. Requires knowing _____.

   C. Requires knowing _____.

IV. Perspective for Pursuing Christlikeness

   A. Requires _____.

   B. Requires _____.

   C. Requires _____.

   D. Requires _____.

V. Perspective for Perfected Citizenship

   A. Comes from _____.

   B. Comes from _____.

   C. Comes from _____.

Heaven-Focused
MINDSET

HEAVEN-FOCUSED MINDSET
Day 1

This week you'll study Philippians 3 designed to help you focus on cultivating "there and then" thinking. If our life is represented by the dash on our grave marker, we want to make it count! I discuss this in the Heaven-focused Mindset video lesson. Visit www.elizabethmahusay.com to access the video and fill in your listening guide.

Today we look at our fourth Mindset demonstrated by Paul. List the three Mindsets you have already studied.

1. _____.

2. _____.

3. _____.

Pray and ask God to open your heart and mind to the truth of His Word today. Read Philippians 3.

Paul shows us how a "Heaven-focused" Mindset gives us perspective. List the five areas of perspective that I share in the video lesson.

1. _____.

2. _____.

3. _____.

4. _____.

5. _____.

Due to the influence of various false teachers, the Philippian believers begin to question the genuineness of their salvation. Some of these false teachers proclaim that salvation is guaranteed through earthly rituals, ceremony, and legalism. To combat this, Paul writes to remind the Philippians that salvation comes through Christ alone. "To write the same things again is no trouble to me, and it is a safeguard for you" (verse 1). The "same things" refers back to Philippians 1:27-28, where Paul exhorts the believers to "conduct themselves in a manner worthy" and encourages them to be "in no way alarmed by your opponents." Paul wants the Philippian believers to be certain of their salvation.

1. Despite their present circumstances, what does Paul encourage the Philippians to do in verse 1?

2. Why is it so important to base our joy in the Lord rather than on our circumstances?

3. Has your attitude reflected joy lately? If not, what has hindered you?

4. According to John 15:11, what is Jesus' desire for believers?

In Philippians 3:2, Paul warns the Philippians about their opponents. He describes these false teachers as "dogs, evil workers, and mutilators of the flesh." Let's look at each one of these descriptors.

Paul's use of "dogs" refers to the wild, four-legged scavengers that plagued ancient cities by roaming in packs and attacking humans.

5. How does Revelation 22:15 describe "dogs"?

Paul describes the false teachers as "evil workers" because they base their work on selfish pride and not on a desire to bring glory to God. These false teachers were directly attacking the Philippian believers with a salvation by works message.

6. How does II John 1:9-11 tell us to react to evil workers or false teachers?

"Beware of mutilation" refers to a twisted form of legalism in which Jews declare that circumcision and keeping the customs of Moses are necessary for someone to be saved (Acts 15:1). God introduces circumcision in Genesis 17:10 as a sign of His covenant with Abraham and his descendants. Paul's point here is that circumcision is not necessary for salvation.

7. What kind of circumcision is important to the Lord, according to Romans 2:29?

As I think about circumcision of the heart, I am reminded of a passage of scripture I often pray over myself and my family. Look up Deuteronomy 30:6 and record it below.

We are each called to love the Lord our God with all our heart and with all our soul. This is only possible if we allow God to circumcise or "cut out" those things that are not honoring to Him. As we submit to the skillful hand of God we experience the life that God intends for us.

8. In thinking about your present circumstances and how you respond to them, what do you need God to circumcise in your heart today?

Much like the false teachers of Paul's day, we live in a world that can cause us to question our salvation. We are bombarded 24/7 with messages that we're "not enough." Who we are is not enough, how we look is not enough, and what we have is not enough, to name a few. Dwell on these thoughts of "not enough" for an extended time and we can start to believe that these lies are true.

9. Ephesians 2:8-10 provides a clear picture of the basis of salvation. Look at these verses and record what you learn.

Journal today about common cultural messages delivered as truth that you recognize to be lies.

HEAVEN-FOCUSED MINDSET
Day 2

READ PHILIPPIANS 3:1-6.

I am definitely an achievement-oriented person. I enjoy working, and I am especially willing to work hard to achieve that "next thing." For many years I lived a life built on my achievements: honor roll throughout school, graduating third in my high school class, graduating with honors from University of South Florida with a bachelor's and master's of education, enjoying a satisfying teaching career, and then building my successful home-based business.

What I came to realize is that these achievements never satisfied me. I found myself always looking for the *next* thing to achieve. I knew the Lord, but I was not living my life to glorify God. Rather, I was living to bring glory to myself. My confidence was in my flesh. But a fleshly confidence produces an "Earth-focused" Mindset. I needed to cultivate a "Heaven-focused" Mindset — which Paul reminds the Philippian believers in his letter.

Paul examines his own life in an autobiographical way, to see what he has of worth and value. He discovers that he has nothing! Paul reinforces the point he made in verse 3: that true believers do not place confidence in their flesh, but in Jesus.

1. Fill out the chart below by listing Paul's credentials based on his birth (verse 5), and his credentials based on his achievements (verses 5-6).

Paul's Credentials

Based on Birth	Based on Achievement
1.	1.
2.	2.
3.	3.
	4.

Let's look more closely at Paul's achievements, to gain a greater under-standing of why he thought them worthy of mention.

In calling himself a "Hebrew of Hebrews," Paul shares that he achieved manhood without forsaking the Hebrew customs and family traditions taught to him by his parents. Unlike Paul, many Jews had assimilated into the Greco-Roman culture.

Paul then shares that he had once been a highly respected Pharisee, a member of an elite, influential, and well-respected group of men that metic-ulously lived to know, interpret, guard, and obey the Law.

2. What does Jesus tell us about the Pharisees in Matthew 15:8-9, 14?

Paul shares that his once zealous persecution of the Church was based on his intense love for God. Paul was sincere in his religious beliefs, but his actions were wrong. Paul's actions prove that religious zeal can be misguided.

3. From Acts 26:9-11, name ways that Paul persecuted the Church.

Lastly, Paul shares that he had achieved a seemingly faultless life via outward conformity to the Law. Because he adhered to the Law and Jewish tradition perfectly, Paul's behavior was deemed blameless by those observing him. Yet after coming to know Jesus as Savior, Paul asserts in Galatians 2:21 that "if righteousness comes through the Law, then Christ died needlessly." Our outward conformity to the laws and traditions of our religion cannot save us.

4. As you audit your own life, what are some things about you, based on birth and/or achievement, that could give you a false sense of confidence?

Ladies, I began this lesson by sharing earthly things in which I *could* place my confidence. But having an "Earth-focused" Mindset made me too sensitive to how others viewed me. Caring more about the "here and now" of my earthly living, rather than the "there and then" of my heavenly home, imprisoned me to a narrow view of my life. But as God has transformed my thinking to a "Heaven-focused" Mindset, I find that I am less chained by the opinions — and expectations — of others. I am learning daily to focus on yielding to Him and the accomplishment of His plan for my life. Then and only then can I experience true fulfillment.

> CARING MORE ABOUT THE "HERE AND NOW" OF MY EARTHLY LIVING, RATHER THAN THE "THERE AND THEN" OF MY HEAVENLY HOME, IMPRISONED ME TO A NARROW VIEW OF MY LIFE.

Journal today by recording thoughts that dominate your thinking about your "here and now."

_____

_____

_____

_____

_____

_____

_____

_____

_____

HEAVEN-FOCUSED MINDSET
Day 3

READ PHILIPPIANS 3:1-11.

Recall that Paul is writing as though he is an accounting auditor. After counting up his gains, he determines that he's bankrupt! A "Heaven-focused" Mindset provides perspective for purposed counting. As a review of yesterday's credentials, let's look at how Paul valued his gains/losses in view of Christ.

Things Paul Counted as Gain	Things Paul Counted as Loss
Circumcised the eighth day	Ritual
+ Of the nation of Israel	+ Race
+ Of the tribe of Benjamin	+ Rank
+ A "Hebrew of Hebrews"	+ Family tradition
+ A Pharisee	+ Membership
+ Zealous persecutor of the church	+ Sincerity of belief
+ Righteous according to the Law	+ Outward conformity to rules
= **Profit for Paul.** **Paul's confidence in himself.**	= **Bankruptcy for Paul.** **Paul's confidence in Christ.**

1. According to verse 8, what else does Paul consider a loss compared to knowing Christ? How does he count his achievements in order to gain Christ?

In verses 7 and 8 Paul transitions from his past thinking to his present thinking. "But whatever things were gain to me, those things I have counted as loss for the sake of Christ," he writes. "Yet indeed I also count all things loss for the excellence of the knowledge of Christ Jesus my Lord." Paul's thinking is so dramatically transformed by his faith in Jesus Christ, that he begins to count all else to be loss.

2. In light of the scriptures you studied in Day 2 and today, what do you think it means to count all things as loss, compared to knowing Christ?

3. What are some practical things a believer must do to grow her faith to count all other things as loss?

4. List people, things, accomplishments, dreams, etc., that you value.

5. Do you value anything you listed above more than you value Christ?

6. What do you think hinders us from counting things as loss?

Paul makes the choice to disregard his achievements, so that he might take hold of the surpassing benefits of knowing Christ. It is from this privilege of knowing Jesus, that Paul gladly suffers the loss of all things. Again, "all things" refers to anything he might use to earn salvation apart from Christ. Paul goes so far as to call these things "rubbish," which is a strong word that means "waste," "dung," "manure," or even "excrement." I imagine the stench, the flies, and the disgust of never being able to get away from such wretchedness!

7. Use verse 9 to fill in the blanks, to see the thinking Paul rejects to replace with truth. Note: I have used the New King James version.

"...Not having _____ righteousness, which is from the

_____, but that which is through _____ in

Christ, the righteousness which is from _____ by

_____."

Paul had spent much of his life working to achieve righteousness. But it was self-righteousness, and it left his account empty. When Paul chooses to trust Christ, he sets aside his own self-righteousness to gain the righteousness of Christ. In effect, Christ transfers His righteousness to Paul's spiritually bankrupt "account." Ladies, Christ does the same for us!

8. Read verse 10. What three things does Paul want to know?

1. _____.

2. _____.

3. _____.

Paul clearly understands that the more he knows Christ, the more His resurrection power will manifest itself in Paul's life. Ladies, like Paul, we need to grow in our knowledge of Christ to experience His power. *It is this power that gives us everything we need for life and godliness!* Christ desires a personal relationship with us so that we might effectively appropriate His resurrection power in our lives.

> IT IS THIS POWER THAT GIVES US EVERYTHING WE NEED FOR LIFE AND GODLINESS!

Christ's resurrection stands as the greatest display of Christ's power, because it demonstrates His absolute authority over both the physical and spiritual realms. (Colossians 2:14-15, 1 Peter 3:18-20).

9. What does II Peter 1:3 tell us Christ's divine power gives us?

The challenge for me, personally, is my acceptance of the word "everything." Because "everything" includes the mountain top highs and the valley lows. "Everything" encompasses the attacks of the enemy, and the suffering that results from living in our fallen world.

Throughout his writing, Paul shares his highs and his lows. He shares the joys of ministry as well as the persecution by those who hate him. This suffering results simply from his choice to follow Jesus. Will you and I also suffer simply because we follow Jesus? Some examples of suffering that you and I might have to endure:

- Being sued for choosing not to serve someone through your business, because doing so violates your Christian beliefs.
- Being denied government funding unless images of the Ten Commandments or portraits of Jesus are removed.
- Being told you may not have a Bible openly displayed on your desk at work.
- Being terminated from your job for openly sharing your faith with a co-worker.
- Losing friends who disagree with your biblical stance on issues.

10. Have you suffered recently? Briefly describe this trail and name one lesson you have learned through your struggle?

The good news is that just like Paul, we are not alone. As you will recall, fellowship means "to be in partnership" with someone. Christ is always in fellowship with us, encouraging and empowering us for the suffering we must endure on our journey. A good question we can ask ourselves is, "What kind of partner am I?" God is worthy of partners that persevere, are loyal, and willing to say, "Not my will, but Yours be done."

II Peter 1:5-8 encourages us to supplement our faith with virtue, knowledge, self-control, perseverance, godliness, brotherly kindness, and love so that we are the most productive and useful in our knowledge of Christ! As we do our part to fellowship with God by supplementing our faith, we more effectively grow in the knowledge of God. This growth means a greater appropriation of God's resurrection power, which is exactly what we need to endure the trials of life.

11. What does James 1:2-4,12 say about the benefits of trials?

12. The word "trial" in James 1 could also be translated "temptation." What does I Corinthians 10:13 tell us about temptation?

Having a Heaven-focused Mindset means also having a Christ-like Mindset. Jesus suffered on His journey to the cross because He was confident in His return to Heaven. In his commentary on Philippians, J.A. Motyer states, "We must be ready for — and we cannot hope to avoid — the downward path of the Crucified. This is the way the Lord Jesus went, and it is the way of Christlikeness for us."[7] I immediately think of Galatians 2:20, which says "I have been crucified with Christ; it is no longer I who live, but Christ lives in me."

We must choose to be crucified with Christ in order to cultivate a Heaven-focused Mindset and attain resurrection from death (verse 11). Christ knew that after the resurrection came ascension. Ascension meant returning to His rightful place at the right hand of His Father in Heaven. We, too, have the promise of a heavenly home and eternity in the presence of our heavenly Father! May our Heaven-focused Mindset compel us to suffer well for the sake of the Gospel.

Below are questions I have asked myself in my journey toward having a Heaven-focused Mindset. As you read them, consider how you would answer based on where you are now in your walk with Christ.

How badly do you want to be like Christ?

As the Lord was preparing me to teach women's Bible studies I suffered extensive spiritual warfare. My husband, Fred, was instrumental in supporting me and encouraging me during this season. His suggestion for me to give up teaching science was a turning point in my life. People ask me all the time if I miss teaching science and I joyfully tell them, "No, because I'm still teaching, just a different subject."

When suffering comes through the loss of someone or something you love, are you willing to trust God in order to gain Christ?

Fred and I have experienced many losses in our lives. I remember our first pregnancy. We were so excited and so ready to be parents. I had a miscarriage at 14 weeks and it devastated us. I didn't understand but I trusted God was at work. Fred, in the process of working through his grief, accepted Christ as his Savior! That devastating loss lead to Heavenly gain!

Are you willing to leave behind all the things you've worked so hard for in this life?

As Fred and I sensed God calling us to leave our home in Florida and move 1100 miles west to Texas, we knew we were giving up closeness to family, established friendships, successful ministry, and extensive business contacts. When we drove away from the home we loved and headed west we both agreed there was no looking back.

Are you willing to walk in obedience even if it means suffering?

As we began to rebuild our lives in Texas, we endured much suffering. We suffered through feelings of aloneness, isolation, and questioning of our decision. We suffered through financial hardship as the realities of rebuilding our businesses hit. We suffered rejection from people who didn't understand why we would move and restart. We kept getting up every day and going to work regardless of how we felt, trusting God to provide all that we needed. He has done exceedingly and abundantly more in our lives. God is faithful!

Are you willing to set your mind on the things above, not on earthly things (Colossians 3:2)?

In each of the above examples from my life, Fred and I did not respond perfectly. We made mistakes. We had moments of anger with God and even questioned His ways. I cried. We cried together. Through it all God refined us — and still is. I am still learning how to set my mind on things above.

But because of our faithfulness, we now have two established businesses in Texas. We have made countless friends. And technology enables us to encourage people all over the world through our Rock My Marriage Ministry. Every Monday we go live on Facebook for #MarriageMattersMonday, to share our struggles, victories, and how God is working in our marriage. The last 20 years have been an amazing journey and I am eternally grateful for the countless opportunities God has provided to cultivate a Heaven-focused Mindset in both of us.

Journal today with your responses to the above questions. What fears come to mind as you consider them? What victories come to mind?

HEAVEN-FOCUSED MINDSET
Day 4

READ PHILIPPIANS 3:1-16.

Paul's goal, as stated in verse 10, is to know Christ and the power of His resurrection and the fellowship of His sufferings.

In verses 12-16, Paul shares how he is still actively pursuing that goal. In his process of doing so, we find perspective for our own pursuit of Christ. Paul relates this to a race; he is an athlete pressing toward the finish line for the prize. The purpose is to pursue Christlikeness, and the prize is spiritual perfection. While we will never fully realize spiritual perfection this side of heaven, we can and must continue to grow spiritually if we are to experience the life of joy that God intends for us.

I admit it is a struggle for me to focus on heavenly reward more than earthly achievement. After all, I like achieving. I like to have a sense of accomplishment. I like to appear perfect on my own merit. So trust me when I say that I have to remind myself often that I need God's Word to help me cultivate a Heaven-focused Mindset. Then and only then can I focus on what matters most.

1. According to verse 12, Paul is not perfected. Do you ever feel the need to pretend to be perfect? If so, why?

To grow spiritually, we must first recognize that our perfection is not the goal. As believers, we need a healthy discontentment with where we are in our spiritual walk. We must continue to eliminate sin and cultivate holiness. It is out of our awareness of our spiritual condition that we will desire to pursue the prize.

As the power of the Spirit is released in our lives, we develop a super sensitive awareness of our sins, which produces humility before God. Many Christians are self-satisfied in their race because they compare themselves to other Christians with less progress in being Christ-like. Had Paul compared himself with others, he would likely have been tempted to be proud and perhaps let up a bit.

2. Are there areas of your Christian walk that you can admit you are self-satisfied?

I entered adulthood not realizing that I strongly projected an "I am perfect" image. I wanted others to think I had it all together. As a result, I rarely shared any of my personal struggles in life, business, or relationships. I was only transparent with those closest to me — and even then only sparingly. In effect, I was being dishonest! I knew that I had sin and flaws, wrong thinking, and sometimes made poor decisions. In essence, I was living a lie.

3. What does Jeremiah 9:5 have to say about lying?

I had to break the sinful habit of lying, beginning with my thinking that I was fooling God and others about who I really was. I needed to be transparent with God, myself, and everyone else.

4. In Psalm 139:23-24, David is transparent before God. What three things does David ask God to do?

   1. _____

   2. _____

   3. _____

I believe that when we ask, God reveals our spiritual state. Because of our sinful, human natures, we tend to determine our level of spirituality by comparing ourselves to others. Will you admit to doing this — perhaps on a daily basis? I sure will! But there are dangers in comparison. One is becoming insensitive to the sin in our life that needs to go. When we look to someone we deem spiritually less mature, we can become prideful. On the other hand, if we compare ourselves to more mature Christians, we are in danger of thinking that we are worse than we are.

Comparison with others is a changing standard and it is detrimental to our mind. For example, when I first starting writing Bible studies I was in

COMPARISON WITH OTHERS IS A CHANGING STANDARD AND IT IS DETRIMENTAL TO OUR MIND.

the habit of comparing myself to another well-known teacher at our church. In my comparison, she was more educated and had more experience writing and teaching studies at our church. The more I dwelled on her, the more insecure I became in my writing and preparation for teaching. My lack of confidence and fear of failing almost stalled my effectiveness for Christ. I am so thankful for the mentor who encouraged me to get my eyes off her, and to look to God's standard as I work to please Him in all I do.

Ladies, only God's standard is constant and perfectly designed to mold each of us into the likeness of Christ. His Word equips us for the accomplishment of His perfect will. Like Paul, we must "press on" each day. When Paul writes that he will "press on," he commits to an active, aggressive, diligent pursuit. Paul's goal is to catch the very reason for which Christ Jesus had come to save him: to conform Paul to Christ's image. To effectively pursue the prize of "spiritual perfection," we also must focus on becoming like Christ. Ladies, this is our life-long purpose.

5. On a scale of 1 to 10, with 10 being the most diligent, honestly rate your pursuit of a life devoted to Christ.

6. What, if anything, is hindering your pursuit?

7. Had Paul reached the goal of Christlikeness, according to verse 13?

8. What two action steps does Paul share in order to reach his goal?

Paul maintains his focus by forgetting those things that lie behind. "Forgetting" does not mean "failing to remember." It means no longer being influenced by or affected by our past. Hallelujah!

Ladies, it is critical that we deal with our sin problem in the present. As we run our race for Christlikeness, we cannot ignore sin and pretend that it doesn't matter. Satan will use unconfessed sin as a weapon to knock us out of the race. Confess sin immediately; learn from your failures and successes, and continually look ahead. Don't let Satan convince you that your sins are too big for Christ to forgive. They're not!

Here are some passages of Scripture to encourage us in this.

"If we confess our sins, He is faithful and just to forgive us our sins and to cleanse us from all unrighteousness." (1 John 1:9)

"As far as the east is from the west, so far has He removed our transgressions from us." (Psalm 103:12)

"Have mercy upon me, O God, according to Your lovingkindness; according to the multitude of Your tender mercies, blot out my transgressions. Wash me thoroughly from my iniquity, and cleanse me from my sin. For I acknowledge my transgressions, and my sin is always before me...Create in me a clean heart, O God, and renew a steadfast spirit within me." (Psalm 51:1-3, 10)

Paul maintains his focus by reaching forward to those things which lie ahead. With perseverance Paul runs swiftly to reach his finish line. Paul's Heaven-focused Mindset keeps him motivated to keep his eye on the prize of spiritual perfection. It is in heaven that Paul knows he will receive "the crown of righteousness" (2 Timothy 4:7-8). The same is true for us!

9. Look back at Philippians 3:13-14. Write out some key thoughts that you can use to cultivate a Heaven-focused Mindset.

In verse 15, Paul encourages all believers with the phrase "as many as are mature." As a Christ-follower, we should share Paul's singular focus of making the maximum effort to pursue Christlikeness.

10. What is Paul's encouragement to believers in verse 16?

Paul encourages the Philippians to consistently live what they already know! As empowered believers of Jesus Christ, they will spend eternity with Him! Their Heaven-focused Mindset empowers them to pursue Christlikeness every day.

May I encourage you to do the same? Keep your eye on the prize of Christlikeness. When the cares of this world weigh you down, run to the Word! When you are thirsty from the race, allow the promises of God to quench your thirst. When the upward climb leaves you feeling breathless, allow God's truths to breathe life into your lungs. When thoughts of quitting clutter your mind, clearly hear the voice of God's saints cheering you over the finish line!

Some Scriptures of encouragement!

"Do you not know that those who run in a race all run, but one receives the prize? Run in such a way that you may obtain it" (1 Corinthians 9:24).

"Holding fast the word of life, so that I may rejoice in the day of Christ that I have not run in vain or labored in vain" (Philippians 2:16).

"Blessed are those who hunger and thirst for righteousness, for they shall be satisfied" (Matthew 5:6).

"All Scripture is God-breathed and is useful for teaching, rebuking, correcting and training in righteousness" (2 Timothy 3:16 NIV).

"Therefore we also, since we are surrounded by so great a cloud of witnesses, let us lay aside every weight, and the sin which so easily ensnares us, and let us run with endurance the race that is set before us, looking unto Jesus, the author and finisher of our faith, who for the joy that was set before Him endured the cross, despising the shame, and has sat down at the right hand of the throne of God" (Hebrews 12:1-2).

Journal today with thoughts about your heavenly home. How does heaven encourage you to pursue Christlikeness more passionately?

_____

_____

_____

_____

_____

_____

_____

_____

HEAVEN-FOCUSED MINDSET
Day 5

READ PHILIPPIANS 3:1-21.

In the final segment of his letter, Paul encourages the Philippian believers to know where their home is. A Heaven-focused Mindset provides perspective for perfected citizenship. Paul's goal is for Philippians to change their thinking and redirect their focus from earthly things to heavenly things. From their flawed earthly citizenship to their perfected heavenly citizenship. As modern believers, we share in Paul's goal. One of the first steps in changing our focus is to find godly examples.

    1. What encouragement does Paul give the Philippian believers in verse 17?

Paul clearly establishes that he is not perfect, but pursuing perfection. This makes him an example we can follow. He shows us how to overcome our imperfections; how to handle life's struggles, disappointments, and trials; and how to handle pride, resist temptation, and put sin to death.

    2. Do you have believers in your life who model a Christ-like example? What about them encourages you to press on to be more like Christ?

In verses 17 and 18 Paul draws contrast between godly examples — "note those who so walk, as you have us for a pattern," and ungodly examples — those he weeps over as "the enemies of the cross of Christ." He weeps because they are not saved and face destruction. He weeps because they are focused on earthly things that make them devoted to self-indulgence. "Whose god is their appetite or belly" (verse 19) is a metaphor that refers to all unrestrained sensual, fleshly, and bodily desire. (See 1 Corinthians 6:13). This leads to exaltation of things and practices that should bring them shame, *not* glory or boasting.

   3. Do you know anyone who is an "enemy of the cross"? Take some time to pray for them. Read Matthew 28:19-20. What is Jesus commissioning you to do?

   4. Per verse 20, with what attitude should we be awaiting our Savior's return? What is your current attitude toward His return?

Ladies, let's pursue Christlikeness because our perfected citizenship is in heaven. When we cultivate a Heaven-focused Mindset, we earnestly long for Christ to return and take us to be with Him! (See 1 Thessalonians 4:17). We live on earth but our home in heaven must dominate our thinking. We can have joy today because we know He is coming! I can have contentment with what I have now, because I see beyond to what I will have in my future heavenly home.

   5. What happens to our body upon Christ's return (verse 21)?

   6. Use verse 21 to describe Christ's power.

As believers, we will some day cross the finish line of our life's race. Verse 21 assures us of a glorious thing: that our lowly bodies will be transformed to be like Christ's. God's almighty power will make us spiritually perfect and conform us to the image of His Son! (Romans 8:29, 1 John 3:2).

Chapter 3 is a laser shining in our lives. Just as a laser cuts through the thickest of material, God's Word can cut away those "nice things" in our lives that obscure our focus on Christ and our heavenly home.

When "things" dominate our thinking more than Christ, our focus becomes materialistic, self-centered, and ambitious. God calls us to be spiritually minded, not focused on obtaining status or material things. Bible commentator Warren Weirsbe states it this way: "People who live for 'things' are never really happy because they must constantly protect their treasures and worry lest they lose their value. Not so for the believer with the spiritual mind; her treasure in Christ can never be stolen and they never lose their value."[8]

Ladies, let us each eagerly seek Christ for direction, wisdom, and discernment, and allow Him to become the guiding force in our life!

8. Time for you to get real: Is your future reward in heaven more important than your earthly achievements?

Today I'd like you to journal after you've spent a bit of time in God's presence. Is God prompting you to seek a Heaven-focused Mindset? If so, what is He saying to you?

Week 5

INTENTIONALITY MINDSET

LISTENING GUIDE
Philippians 4: 1-9

I. Intentionally Stand:

    A. In _____.

    B. With _____.

    C. With _____.

II. Intentionally Pray:

    A. With _____ and _____.

    B. Without _____ but with _____.

III. Intentionally Think:

Conscious mind facts: _____.

Unconscious mind facts: _____.

Five Steps to Retrain Your Brain:

1. Embrace the need to _____.

2. Consider your _____.

3. _____ wrong thinking and _____ with truth.

4. Repeat the process with passion and _____.

5. Find and submit to _____.

IV. Intentionally Live:

_____

_____

_____

Philippians 4:8

True: Word of God
Noble: Worthy of respect
Just: What is fair
Pure: Clean from every fault, from carnality, and chaste
Lovely: Beautiful, attractive
Good Report: Positive and constructive
Virtue: Moral excellence
Praiseworthy: Worthy of commending to others

Scriptures in Philippians useful for replacing wrong thoughts:

Thoughts to Reject	Truths to Claim
Things will never change for the better in my life.	God promises to complete the work He began in me. (Philippians 1:6)
I am fed up with these other believers.	God desires that I love other believers and bring Him glory. (Philippians 1:9-11, 21)
I just do not get why they will not follow my lead!	God desires that I have a submissive, humble mind (like Christ) that thinks of others more. (Philippians 2:3-5)
I am sick and tired of _____.	God commands me to do all things without complaining and disputing, so that I can be His light. (Philippians 2:14-15)
Look at all that I have accomplished!	God desires that I put no confidence in my flesh. (Philippians 3:7-8)
There is no point in continuing to fight for right thinking.	God desires that I know my purpose of becoming Christ-like. (Philippians 3:12-14)
Does it matter if it goes against the Bible. Everyone else is doing it!	God desires that I set my mind on heavenly things, not earthly things. (Philippians 3:18-20)
I am so worried about _____.	God desires that I not worry, but pray about everything. He promises to guard my heart and mind. (Philippians 4:6-7)
My thoughts are overwhelming me.	God desires that I guard my thoughts by meditating on "these things." (Philippians 4:8)
I cannot make this work anymore. I am tired of fighting.	God promises to be my sufficiency when I am content in Him. (Philippians 4:13)
I do not know how we will ever have enough.	God promises to supply all of my needs when I am in His will. (Philippians 4:19)

Intentionality & God-Confidence MINDSETS

INTENTIONALITY MINDSET
Day 1

This week we turn our attention to the fourth chapter of Philippians. You will spend three days on the Intentionality Mindset designed to help you intentionally choose new ways of thinking. The last two days of your study covers the God-confidence Mindset, which looks at self-confidence versus an unshakeable confidence in God. Visit www.elizabethmahusay.com to access the Intentionality Mindset video and fill in your listening guide.

In my lecture on Intentionality Mindset I focus on Five Steps to Retrain Your Brain. List the five steps below.

1. _____
2. _____
3. _____
4. _____
5. _____

READ PHILIPPIANS 4.

In the first three chapters of Philippians, Paul lays a foundation for our thinking with intentionality. Intentionality means "an instance of determining mentally to act on purpose." Each day presents us with many opportunities to choose how we will react to circumstances and people.

Paul encourages us to have a Gospel Mindset and a No Matter What Mindset in response to our circumstances. He conveys our need to have a Christ-like Everyday Mindset in response to people. And a Heaven-focused Mindset gives us perspective on how to respond to worldly temptations. These Mindsets provide us with the needed foundation to intentionally stand, intentionally pray, intentionally think, and intentionally live.

1. In Philippians 4:1, Paul begins with "therefore," which refers back to what he wrote in Chapter 3. What is Paul's aim? (See also Romans 8:29.)

Paul loves the Philippian believers. They remind him that his work is effective and that the trials and hardships he is enduring are worth it! Out of his love for them, Paul encourages these dear friends to stand firm in the Lord.

2. What does Ephesians 6:10-11 tell us is necessary to be strong in the Lord?

Ephesians 6 uses the phrase "stand against the wiles of the devil." "Wiles" can be translated as "cunning arts, deceit, craft, or trickery." Satan is the master of deceit and trickery.

3. How does 1 Peter 5:8 describe the devil? What are we to do, according to 1 Peter 5:9?

One of the "wiles of the devil" is disunity. Our enemy knows that if he can drive a wedge between believers he can potentially splinter the message of the Gospel. In Philippians 4:2, Paul pleads with Euodia and Syntyche "to live in harmony in the Lord." Paul knows that if they live in right relationship with the Lord, they will be in right relationship with each other. Their salvation will provide a common ground for unity.

The disagreement between these two women appears serious, because Paul asks a "true companion" to help them resolve the issue. He recognizes that continued disharmony between them will be tragic for the Philippian church. The same is still true today. Have you seen church members drive a church apart?

4. Pray and ask the Lord to reveal any dispute you might have with another person that you need to address today. What action steps can you take to heal your relationship?

Review your answers in the "Journal today" section of the *Gospel Mindset* lesson from week one. Reread and ponder what you wrote, filtering each of your answers through biblical truth. Label each thought with the word REJECT or KEEP. (I suggest using a different colored pen). If you label an answer with REJECT, write out a substitutionary biblical truth. This can be a direct scripture or a thought based on biblical truth.

For example:
Day 1: Record some of the thoughts you believe keep you from freely sharing the Gospel.

The thought I recorded: "I don't have the time." REJECT

Substitutionary biblical truth: Lord help me to "make the best use of my time, because the days are evil" and people need to know the salvation of the Lord today. Ephesians 5:16

INTENTIONALITY MINDSET
Day 2

READ PHILIPPIANS 4:1-7.

Paul now turns his attention to the need for intentional prayer. He addresses both the heart (our feelings) and the mind (our thinking). Verses 4-6 give us a step-by-step approach to inner peace: rejoice in the Lord always (4:4), be gentle (4:5), be aware of God's divine presence (4:5), don't be anxious about anything (4:6), and pray about everything (4:6).

Step one of Paul's approach is to rejoice.

"Rejoice in the Lord always; again I will say, rejoice!" (Philippians 4:4). Rejoicing gives strength to the people of God. (Nehemiah 8:10, Proverbs 15:13). Paul uses a repeat for added emphasis, which could mean that he knows it is not always easy to be joyful.

But joy is not an emotion or feeling, ladies! And we must stop treating it as such. Neither is it happiness, which is a feeling based on an attitude of satisfaction in favorable circumstances. In contrast, joy is our confidence that God is securely in control of all things for our good and His glory. As a result, we can have joy, no matter our circumstances!

This God-confidence is what allows a person who has lost a loved one to have joy in spite of sorrow. When our rejoicing is a continual, habitual practice, we can rejoice in all things. But ladies, this is only possible when we base our joy on the only sure, reliable, unwavering, and unchanging source of joy: God.

I was thankful for this truth about joy the fall my dad's health took a sharp decline. I remember the phone call telling me that he was in hospice care — and might only live a few more days. I was 1100 miles away! I remember that feeling in my gut as I thought, "No! I am not ready for my dad to die." Fortunately, he bounced back and was able to celebrate his 70th birthday.

But in the midst of dad's declining health, I was experiencing joy as we celebrated our oldest son's senior year activities. Fred and I attended his band competitions, proudly walked across the field for Senior Recognition Night, and planned our son's next steps beyond high school. Of course, I was in constant communication with my step-mom about dad. It was such an emotional roller coaster. I was having to walk in the truth that God's plan for my dad was perfect, while helping my step-mom say good-bye to the love of her life. Dad died just several weeks later.

DEATH IS HARD, BUT THE JOY OF KNOWING I WILL SEE MY DAD AGAIN IS GREATER!

Death is hard, but the joy of knowing I will see my dad again is greater! I was reminded of the King James Version of 1 Corinthians 15:55: "O death, where is your sting? O grave, where is your victory?" Through Christ, my dad has victory over the grave, and I rejoice in the truth that I will see him again in heaven.

1. Is it a habit in your life to always rejoice in the Lord? What situations threaten to prevent you from always rejoicing?

Step two of Paul's approach is to exhibit gentleness to all people.

Gentleness refers to graciousness of humility. The type of humble graciousness that produces the patience needed to endure being wrongly treated and/or disgraced without retaliation, bitterness, or vengeance. Instead of self-love, it is our choosing to love others. Instead of self-esteem, based on our own self-assessment, it is God-esteem, based on how we measure up to God's unchanging standards.

My 22 years of marriage have afforded me many opportunities to practice gracious humility. Fred and I started dating in high school, so we have spent the last 31 years growing and maturing together. We are both strong-willed, opinionated, and passionate in our desire to be right. We have both made mistakes in how we have treated the other. We each brought very different baggage into our relationship. Fred's mother, for example, died when he was eight. My parent's divorced when I was two.

Understanding each other is work. I *work* to respect Fred and he *works* to love me the way God commands. (Ephesians 5:33.) It is humbling to realize that apart from God's grace and empowerment, we are incapable of fulfilling this command. This realization drives us to cultivate God-esteem more than self-esteem as we measure our lives according to His unchanging standard.

2. Name some ways you can demonstrate humble graciousness to:

a. Your co-workers:

b. Your spouse:

c. Your children:

d. Other:

Step three of Paul's approach is to cultivate a sensitivity to the presence of Jesus Christ.

The word "near" can refer to space or time. The Lord can be near because Christ will soon return (Philippians 3:20-21, James 5:7-8) or because when we die, we are ushered into the Lord's presence (Philippians 1:23, 2 Corinthians 5:8). Secondly, "near" can refer to the omnipresence of Christ.

He is present with believers at all times and in all circumstances (Matthew 28:20). Jesus is near to the cry of our hearts; He promises to help and strengthen us. The more we seek to know God by studying and meditating on His Word, the more we will think about His nearness. The more we encourage this thinking to pervade our life, the more our attitude will be characterized by joy. The more our attitude is characterized by joy, the more our actions reflect that joy. The more we act on this joy, the more effectively we combat anxiety. What's not to love about that?!

3. Do you struggle with joy? What causes you anxiety on a regular basis?

Step four of Paul's approach is to be anxious for nothing.

Ladies, we are to "not worry about anything"! The word "anxious" in this phrase means to "be pulled in different directions." Do you not often feel pulled apart by the struggle between our hopes and our fears? I know I do!

Worry has far-reaching consequences; not just physically, but mentally and emotionally. Headaches, neck pains, ulcers, and back pains are only a few areas our body can be affected by worry. Worry can negatively impact our thinking, our digestion, and even our coordination. There are thousands of drugs to treat the symptoms of worry, but not one can remove its cause. Worry is an inside job.

An area of my life that has often caused me to feel "pulled in different directions" is finances. I have experienced a lot of anxiety over money or lack of money in my life. When I was in college, I worried about my scholarship being enough to pay all of my school expenses. Early in my marriage, I worried how my husband and I would pay for home repairs. After we both became fully self-employed, our fluctuating income caused me to worry about having enough money to pay all of our monthly obligations.

In each of those scenarios, however, I had wrong thinking and wrong feeling. I thought that it was all up to me to cover my needs. Some days I felt overly confident, but some days I felt completely overwhelmed.

Worry, you see, is false care caused by a lack of faith and by a wrong set of values and priorities.

> WORRY, YOU SEE, IS FALSE CARE CAUSED BY A LACK OF FAITH AND BY A WRONG SET OF VALUES AND PRIORITIES.

I cared more about how I would pay for things than I cared about glorifying God in my life. I valued my convenience more than I valued developing patient endurance as God worked on my behalf. Worry grows out of our unbelief that God will keep His promises. Like weeds, worry chokes the application of God's Word in our lives.

4. According to verse 6, what is God's prescription for dealing with anxiety?

The final step of Paul's approach is prayer.

"But in everything, by prayer and supplication, with thanksgiving, let your request be made known to God" (Philippians 4:6). Prayer is the general term for making our requests known to the Lord. Here, it specifically relates to our adoration, devotion, and worship to the Lord.

When you feel overwhelmed, fall on your face before the Lord and worship Him. We must know that He is big enough to solve ALL of our problems. I find that when I spend time in adoration of God, it gives me perspective before I start making requests of Him.

One passage that has helped me to adore God is 1 Chronicles 29:10-13:

> "Blessed are You, Lord God of Israel, our Father, forever and ever. Yours, O Lord, is the greatness, the power and the glory, the victory and the majesty; for all that is in heaven and in earth is Yours; Yours is the kingdom, O Lord, and You are exalted as head over all. Both riches and honor come from You, and You reign over all. In Your hand is power and might; in Your hand it is to make great and to give strength to all. Now therefore, our God, we thank you and praise Your glorious name."

When I am feeling overwhelmed with my circumstances I begin my prayer with this passage. It reminds me that God is able to solve ALL of my problems.

Supplication, sometimes translated as petition, is our desperate cry for help arising from our needs and problems. These supplications are characterized by intensity before the Lord, like the way Jesus prayed in the garden (Hebrews 5:7).

"With thanksgiving" means that we give thanks to God for "all things in the name of our Lord Jesus Christ" (Ephesians 5:20). Our Father likes it when we say "Thank You!"

Ladies, thank God for the answers in advance! Thank God for His loving concern! Thank God for access into His divine presence through Christ's work on the cross!

Would you agree that it is hard to complain when we are thankful? I am learning that my complaints are just worry repackaged. When I complain that there isn't enough time, what I am saying is that I am worried that I won't accomplish the task. By worrying, I am dwelling on my perceived "lack of time," rather than effectively using the time I do have.

5. Why do you think thanksgiving is such a powerful weapon against worry?

6. Name some things for which you are grateful to the Lord today.

7. What will guard your heart and mind (verse 7)?

8. According to Isaiah 26:3, how can we have peace of mind?

Isaiah 26:3 is one of my favorite verses! (the female slant is mine!):

"You will keep her in perfect peace, whose mind is stayed on You, because she trusts in You."

I find myself saying it often, as a reminder of what is necessary to experience peace in the midst of my circumstances. I say aloud, when possible, "God keep me in perfect peace because my mind is stayed on You and I trust You." It requires intentionality on my part to think on God. But it is my responsibility to remind myself of God's faithfulness; that He is a promise keeper, and His plan for my life is perfect.

> BUT IT IS MY RESPONSIBILITY TO REMIND MYSELF OF GOD'S FAITHFULNESS.

Take a moment to look back at your response to question four. Pray intentionally about these things that cause you anxiety. With thanksgiving, earnestly cry to God for help and trust that God is in control of all things in your life. Because He is!

Revisit your "Journal today" responses from No Matter What Mindset, day two. After reviewing them, write at least one circumstance and negative thought response below. Then filter your negative thinking through biblical truth.

Example circumstance: The driver ahead of me is making me late.

Negative Thought Response: This idiot doesn't know how to drive. Ugh…I hate being late!

Biblical Truth: Philippians 2:3-4 encourages me to do nothing out of selfish ambition. A humble mind doesn't call any person an idiot. I'm placing a priority on my interests without considering this person's circumstance or need.

INTENTIONALITY MINDSET
Day 3

READ PHILIPPIANS 4:1-9.

Write out verse 8 below.

I'm not sure that I can adequately convey to you the significance of Philippians 4:8 in my life. After I decided to yield to God and allow Him to begin transforming my thinking, I had no idea how much transformation my thinking needed!

As I began to diligently assess my thinking, Philippians 4:8 became my "go to" filter for whether or not a thought was true. Ladies, I'm not exaggerating when I tell you that in the early days I would quote that scripture 20 to 50 times a day!

My learning to be intentional in my thinking looked something like this:

Thought: "My husband isn't doing anything."

Filter: Is that true, noble, just, pure, lovely, a good report, virtuous, or praiseworthy?

My Response: It certainly isn't worthy of respect, given that he works a full-time job to provide for our family. I reject that thought.

Substitution: Father, you command me to respect my husband (Ephesians 5:33). So I choose right now to respect Fred's commitment to provide for us, and appreciate his need for some downtime when he gets home.

1. To assist in using Philippians 4:8 as a filter, match the virtue with the matching definition.

Virtue	Definition of Virtue
___ True	a. What is fair; conformity to God's standard
___ Noble	b. Worthy of commending to others
___ Just	c. God's Word; opposite of dishonest
___ Pure	d. Excellence; praise, virtue
___ Lovely	e. Well thought of; positive & constructive
___ Good Report	f. Pleasing, attractive; promotes peace
___ Virtue	g. Worthy of respect
___ Praiseworthy	h. Morally pure; wholesome
	Answers: c, g, a, h, f, e, d, b

Let's look at each phrase of this verse.

"Whatever things are true" refers to God's Word. The Bible is true because the "God of truth" inspired it (Psalm 31:5, Isaiah 65:16, Ephesians 4:21). "Thinking on what is true" means reading, analyzing, and meditating on the Word of God.

One of the most important things that I have done in my daily walk is to think differently about the Word of God. I remember hearing a metaphor about viewing the Bible as a table prepared with a feast. It is there before you, but you have to choose to sit down and partake of it.

When I started feasting on the Word of God, viewing it as desirable and fully satisfying (Psalm 19:7-10), I began to see more progress in the transformation of my thinking. God is the author of truth and Satan is the author of lies. The best way to know the truth is to study and memorize scripture as it relates to your life. Only then will you be strong and prepared for the attacks of Satan.

"Whatever things are noble, whatever things are just" refers to what is worthy of respect and what is fair. As everything in God's Word is honorable, meditating on it will move us to think on the eternal and permanent things that are worthy of our awe, adoration, and praise. When we think about earthly things, we tend to focus on the trivial and temporary aspects of life, rather than on the heavenly things that motivate us "to press on" (Philippians 3:12). We should be training our minds to dwell on respectable things, not indecent things.

"Whatever things are pure, whatever things are lovely, whatever things are of good report" refers to thoughts that are morally pure, beautiful, attractive, or worth talking about. Be careful what you allow to enter your mind through watching, reading, and listening. Tabloid magazines that spill the lives of stars for all to read, as well as television programs or movies that promote foul language, adultery, and other immoral behavior can negatively influence our thinking. God will not guard us if we keep opening the door of our heart to the lies of the enemy.

"If there is any virtue and if there is anything praiseworthy" refers to a course of thought characterized by virtuousness and worthwhile in commending to others. This eliminates gossip! Gossip is chatter or idle talk and rumors about the private affairs of others. Gossip can never motivate us to do better, because while we are focusing on someone else's problems we are neglecting to look at our own. Usually gossip is rumor, which means we have not heard the information first-hand. Even if our friend has entrusted us with the private information directly, it is not honorable or right to share it with others. I have learned to ask myself, *"Is what I'm about to share going to make the person hearing it think more highly of the person about whom I am speaking?"* If the answer is no, then I need to not speak.

"Meditate on these things" is meant to stress the idea of a constant thought process. Ladies, we must daily strengthen the moral integrity of our thought life because, as Proverbs 23:7 states, (female emphasis added), "For as she thinks within herself, so she is." Another way to write that is "I must be intentional in my thinking." God's will for us is that we meditate on His Word daily, to fill our hearts and minds with His truth. When we do, we will develop a greater sensitivity for detecting wrong thoughts and develop "great peace" (Psalm 119:165).

> RIGHT THINKING IS THE RESULT OF INTENTIONAL DAILY MEDITATION ON THE WORD OF GOD.

Right thinking is the result of intentional daily meditation on the Word of God.

2. With your group, share how you are applying these virtues or standards in the following areas of your life. Record any changes you need to make in order to better apply them.

Movies you watch:

Music you choose:

TV programs you prefer:

Magazine or books you enjoy:

Conversations in which you participate:

In verse 9, Paul concludes this section with intentional "godly behavior." Godly behavior is rooted in living a life of obedience to God's standards, so that we stand firm when we face difficulty, temptation, and compromise.

To live a more holy life, we must keep our flesh in check. We need to diligently monitor our thoughts to identify those that violate God's standard. We must reject and replace any violations with the truth.

Paul starts Chapter 4 with godly thinking (verses 2-8), which is the prerequisite for godly behavior. Ladies, this is critical: what you think determines the attitudes you possess. The attitudes you possess determine the behaviors you live out. The behaviors you live out determine the example you are for other believers and non-believers. Your example with either attract people to Christ or repel them from Christ.

3. What command does Paul give in verse 9, and what is the blessing that results from obedience to the command?

Paul embodies four important aspects of intentional living in his ministry to the Philippians: "The things which you learned and received and heard and saw in me." "Learned" refers to Paul's teaching, learning, and discipling of the Philippians. He wants the truth of God's Word shared not only "publicly" but also "from house to house" (Acts 20:20). Head knowledge is not enough to effectively live out the Word of God. We must receive it. "Received" refers to taking what is learned as a revelation from God and making it part of who you are (1 Thessalonians 2:13).

When we live out the truth hidden in our heart just like Paul, we provide an example for other believers to follow. "Heard" refers to what the Philippians heard about Paul from other people. "Saw" reminds the Philippians of what they experienced firsthand while Paul was with them. Paul modeled the standard he now writes to them about, as he encourages them to "join in following my example, and note those who so walk, as you have us for a pattern" (Philippians 3:17). We also should be learning, receiving, and hearing so that our living produces a pattern that others can see and follow.

4. Does your living provide a pattern for others to follow? Why or why not?

We are promised that "the God of peace will be with you" when we are obedient to the Word of God. Because God is peace, He is the giver of peace. Paul uses the phrase "God of peace" repeatedly in his writings to remind us that if we have godly thoughts, attitudes, and behaviors, we will be guarded by the peace of God and by the God of peace.

When we "let the peace of God rule in our hearts" (Colossians 3:15), we can expect God to call us out when we have disobeyed. He will not let our disobedience go unnoticed in any area of our lives, because obedience is an essential condition we must meet to have a secure mind and victory over worry.

We have a choice to make: Either we yield our heart and mind to the Spirit of God and practice intentional standing, intentional praying, intentional thinking, and intentional living — or we yield to the flesh and find ourselves wrecked by worry.

An area of my life where this choice is a real struggle is with my sons. As they have grown, I have engaged the battle of yielding my heart and mind to the Spirit of God. It is easy to worry about their choices, their friends, their grades, their jobs, and their future. Yet God continues to remind me that to experience His peace, I need to choose obedience to His way.

I need to intentionally stand in unity with Fred as we parent together. I need to intentionally pray for Anthony and Samuel. Daily prayer empowers me to develop intentional thinking about them. As worry presents itself, I work to filter it through Philippians 4:8 so that I can reject the lies and replace it with the truth of God's Word. Each day is a choice to live intentionally. I so desire to provide a pattern for my boys to follow. This desire challenges me to stay the course in my pursuit of God and in my desire for His Word.

5. Is your life characterized by worry? If yes, where do you need obedience in your life? Take time to repent of the sin of worry and ask God to help you develop obedience to the truth of His Word.

Look back at your "Journal today" responses in Christ-like Everyday Mindset day 3. Reread the thoughts you listed. Filter each thought through the truth of Philippians 4:8. Write REJECT for those revealed as lies, and then write a word or scripture that REPLACES the lie with truth!

GOD-CONFIDENCE MINDSET
Day 4

Yesterday we wrapped up the Intentionality Mindset, and the next two days we spend time considering the God-confidence Mindset.

READ PHILIPPIANS 4:1-16.

In today's world there is such an emphasis on self-confidence. It's interesting to note that when you look up self-confidence, you will find it defined as both a "realistic confidence in one's own judgment or ability" and an "excessive or inflated confidence in one's own judgment or ability." It seems to me that the difference between realistic and excessive is very blurred.

For years, I took pride in my self-confidence. It may have started out as a realistic confidence, but the more I relied on my own judgment and ability, the more I gained an inflated view of my ability and self. I knew the Lord, but I was not placing my confidence in Him. Most of the time I was too busy exerting my self-confidence to even think about what would please God or bring honor and glory to Him. He sat on my shelf; I pulled Him off only after I had exhausted all other options.

> I KNEW THE LORD, BUT I WAS NOT PLACING MY CONFIDENCE IN HIM.

The problem with relying on yourself, however, is that it gets tough to deal with the ups and downs of your life on your own power. So often our circumstances are out of our control; it's easy to feel you're on an emotional roller coaster. If our circumstances are bad, we are sad. We assume people are out to get us and "nothing ever goes my way." If our circumstances are good, we are happy. We reference luck for our good fortune, or affirm what *we* did to bring about these good circumstances. Talk about feeling queasy from an unpredictable ride!

In verses 10-23 Paul begins to make the case for cultivating God-confidence. As God directs us, we need to change what is *within our control* to change. What is *outside of our control* to change requires that we turn these things over to God. We cannot escape the reality of our circumstances, but we can learn from Paul and develop confidence in God's purposes, regardless of our circumstances.

Ladies, I'm about to ask you to get REAL! But before I do, I want to remind you that I daily struggle with self-confidence. Rather than saying, "God can do what He says He can do," I want to say, "I can do what I say I can do!" My challenge is admitting that I can't do everything and that my trying to do so is exhausting. Have you been there, done that, too?

Okay, your turn.

1. Make a mark on the line below that best represents how you currently live your life. Are you more self-confident or God-confident?

   Self-Confident |————————————————————| God-Confident

2. What is a challenging circumstance in your life right now? In this circumstance, are you relying on yourself — or God? Is it an area that He's prompting you to turn over to Him? Tell God the outcome you want, but then leave it at His feet to handle.

Part of Paul's ongoing circumstances includes having his needs met. Note that Paul does not resort to begging God's people to help him. Rather, he presents his needs before the people and then trusts God to meet his needs.

3. What has Paul learned to do in verse 11?

Paul learns to be content. The word "content" in verse 11 means "sufficient for one's self independent of external circumstances," according to *Strong's Exhaustive Bible Concordance*.[10] Some have tried to assert that Paul is promoting human self-reliance. But when taken in context with the verses before and after, Paul uses the word to refer to sufficiency that is based on God's provision.

Christ gives us an endless supply of spiritual resources, which we gain through knowing Him. Paul speaks to these resources in verse 11 when he writes, "Not that I speak in regard to need, for I have *learned* in whatever state I am, to be content." The verb "learned" means "learned by experience."

God takes Paul through many difficult experiences of life to teach him to learn to be content. Paul is saying that we are sufficient, and adequate for the demands of life, because of Christ. The son of God lives within us; we need not depend on outward substitutes.

4. What does verse 13 say is the secret to our contentment?

5. Using Biblegateway.com, look up verse 13. Record the verse here in at least three different versions. Be sure to note the version next to each.

The bottom line is that Paul believes he has all the power necessary to handle life. Do you and I hold the same confidence in God's provision? Will we release this power by faith? We must believe that God is able. Our belief grows out of an intimate, personal, living relationship with our Lord. Ladies, the more dependent we become on God, the more God-confident we become! We can then rely less on ourselves.

> WE MUST BELIEVE THAT GOD IS ABLE.

Look back at your "Journal today" responses for days 2 and 3 of Heaven-focused Mindset. Reread your responses. Answer the questions below.

How is God using your "here and now" to help you *learn* contentment?

_____

_____

_____

Take the fears you listed from day 3 and rewrite them as requests for God to show His power in your life.

GOD-CONFIDENCE MINDSET
Day 5

READ PHILIPPIANS 4:1-23.

Yesterday we learned about Paul being content, no matter his circumstances. Today, let's look at Paul's gratitude for the partnership of the Philippian church in the supplying of his needs.

1. Use verses 15 and 16, to describe how the Philippians give to Paul's ministry.

2. What does Jesus say about giving in Acts 20:35?

3. What is Paul's motivation in receiving a gift from the Philippians (verse 17)?

The Philippians have been generous, and Paul is grateful. Not just for their provision which is now meeting his needs, but also for how God will bless their provision. Paul acknowledges that their gift has brought him joy, not because of what it will "do for him" but on the "return" it gains them. Paul knows that the church will receive spiritually from the Lord for what they have given *materially* to him. Anytime we choose to give to kingdom work, there is a return on our investment. That return is credited to our accounts. Think of it like the interest you earn on an investment account. I believe the interest we receive from our kingdom investments is the joy we share in knowing all that the Lord accomplishes through our resources.

4. What are some ways that you have invested in "kingdom work"? Share any returns on your investment that you have been able to enjoy.

Paul goes on to summarize his joy and gratitude. He tells the Philippians that because of their gift, he has more than enough; that he has been filled up completely (verse 17). Overwhelmed by their generosity, Paul sees their gift as a sacrificial act of worship to God. In Paul's eyes, their gift is a gift from God.

5. What are the three phrases Paul uses to describe the Philippians' gift?

Through Paul's writing in verses 18 and 19, we see the unfolding of one of God's glorious promises. Bible commentator Warren Weirsbe paraphrases Paul when he writes, "You met *my* need, and God is going to meet *your* need. You met *one* need that I have, but my God will meet a*ll* of your needs. You gave out of your *poverty*, but God will supply your needs out of His *riches* in glory!"[9]
God supplies our needs according to His riches in glory by Christ Jesus (verse 19), not "out of His riches." Ladies, His account never decreases! God has a limitless supply of *all that we need* when we are "in Christ Jesus." Jesus is the source of all of God's riches (Colossians 2:3, Ephesians 1:3, 1 Corinthians 1:4-5).

6. What specific need(s) has God met in your life recently? If you can't think of any, I'm going to suggest that you're not looking! God is **always** working for our good!

7. How does knowing that God supplies all of your needs, and that His supply never decreases, encourage you today?

Being entrepreneurs has afforded Fred and I many opportunities to see God supply all of our needs. One of my greatest lessons has been God calling me to wait on His provision rather than working to "make something happen."

I remember an early spring when we were in a tough place financially. Rather than just covering bills with credit, I remember God impressing on me to wait. It definitely wasn't easy for me! A few days later, however, I received an email with a gracious letter detailing how we were receiving an unexpected bonus. I remember falling to my knees in humble adoration of God's provision.

It is important to note that God's promise to supply does not extend to all our greeds. As a child of God, when we are in the will of God, serving for the glory of God, we will have every need met. As author James Hudson Taylor is fond of saying, "God's work done in God's way will never lack God's supply." We can have contentment when we tap into the glorious resources of our God.

Just as the Philippian believers were saints, we are saints "in Christ Jesus" (verse 21). We are called to live as those separated from sin to God for holy purposes. We are to worship, fellowship, have joy, and know our resource, Jesus. He is sufficient.

Conclude today with this closing prayer. Consider making it your daily prayer.

Lord, I offer my life to You to further THE GOSPEL,
NO MATTER WHAT comes my way.

Lord empower me to be CHRIST-LIKE EVERY DAY,
As I maintain a HEAVEN FOCUS.

Lord I choose INTENTIONALITY in my thinking,
So I exude GOD-CONFIDENCE not self-confidence.

Transform my Thinking, God, so that I live a Transformed Life!

GOD-CONFIDENCE MINDSET

LISTENING GUIDE
Philippians 4:10-23

Visit elizabethmahusay.com to access the video.

Confidence: _____

_____

I. Confident in God's Power

    A. Genesis 1:1   Power to _____.

    B. Genesis 35:11   "I am _____."

    C. Psalm 147:5   "_____ is our Lord and

                           _____ in power."

D. 1 Chronicles 29:11   "Yours, O Lord, is the greatness, the

_____..."

E. Isaiah 50:2   His hand isn't shortened...He has power to

_____.

F. Romans 1:16   "Power of God to _____ ..."

G. Ephesians 3:20   His power is at work _____.

H. Philippians 3:20-21   His power is able to _____
all things to Himself.

II. Confident in God's Purpose

A. God's Purpose for Your _____.

B. God's Purpose for Your _____.

C. God's Purpose for Your _____.

III. Confident in God's Provision

A. God's Provision is meant _____.

B. God's Provision meets _____.

C. God's Provision has _____.

D. God's Provision is so _____.

"I SURRENDER ALL"

by Judson Wheeler Van DeVenter

All to Jesus I surrender, All to Him I freely give; I will ever love and trust Him, In His presence daily live.

Chorus:
I surrender all, I surrender all. All to Thee, my blessed Savior, I surrender all.

All to Jesus I surrender, Humbly at His feet I bow, Worldly pleasures all forsaken; Take me, Jesus, take me now.

All to Jesus I surrender, Make me, Savior, wholly Thine; Let me feel Thy Holy Spirit, Truly know that Thou art mine.

All to Jesus I surrender, Lord, I give myself to Thee; Fill me with Thy love and power, Let Thy blessing fall on me.

All to Jesus I surrender, Now I feel the sacred flame. Oh, the joy of full salvation! Glory, glory to His name!

Thoughts I feel God may be calling me to surrender:

_____

_____

_____

_____

_____

_____

_____

_____

_____

_____

TRANSFORM MY THINKING, GOD PRAYER

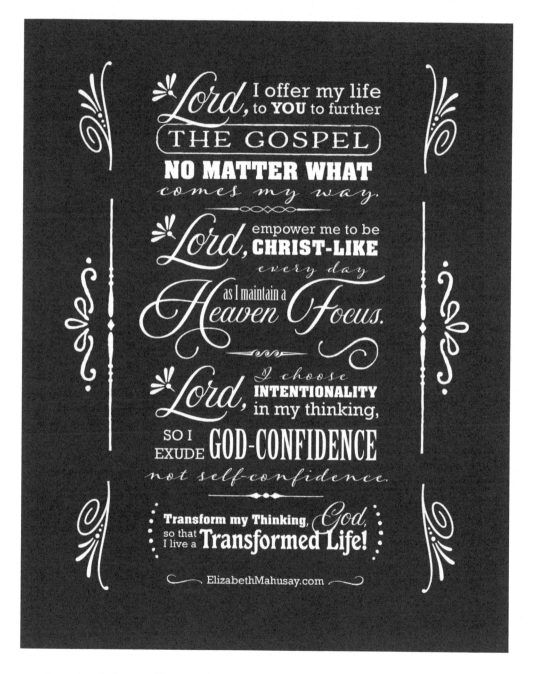

Lord, I offer my life to **YOU** to further THE GOSPEL **NO MATTER WHAT** comes my way.

Lord, empower me to be **CHRIST-LIKE** every day as I maintain a *Heaven Focus.*

Lord, I choose **INTENTIONALITY** in my thinking, SO I EXUDE **GOD-CONFIDENCE** not self-confidence.

Transform my Thinking, *God,* so that I live a **Transformed Life!**

ElizabethMahusay.com

Copies of this wall art can be ordered at www.elizabethmahusay.com.

Through our study of the book of Philippians, we have gained insight into the mind of Paul. Paul had an insatiable hunger to know and experience Jesus Christ. He relied on His grace. He had a mind focused on furthering the Gospel, no matter what life brought his way. His heart's desire was to be Christ-like every day, as he cultivated anticipation for his heavenly home. He was intentional in his thinking and confident that God would see him through.

Paul's challenge to the Philippian church is our challenge today. We are to follow Paul's pattern of thinking which can lead to phenomenal transformation in our lives. At the end of the day, transformed thinking leads to transformed living!

- Will we be open and available for God to use us to further the Gospel?
- Will we trust God no matter what comes our way?
- Will we pursue Christlikeness every day?
- Will we maintain a heavenward focus?
- Will we be intentional in our thinking?
- Will we cultivate God-confidence?

Paul concludes his letter by saying, "The grace of the Lord Jesus Christ be with you all" (verse 23). Paul knows full well the value of God's grace. 2 Corinthians 12:9 states, "My grace is sufficient for you, for My strength is made perfect in weakness." The same grace God offered to Paul, He offers to us. Expect God to graciously answer your heartfelt plea of "Transform My Thinking, God!"

Sisters in Christ, I have so enjoyed taking this journey with you. I look forward to future opportunities to study the Word of God with you. Visit my website www.elizabethmahusay.com to sign up for my newsletter, request me to speak at your location, and learn of upcoming studies. Continue your pursuit of transformed thinking through my Facebook page www.facebook.com/elizabethbmahusay for helpful resources, video encouragement, and accountability.

Serving with Love,

Elizabeth

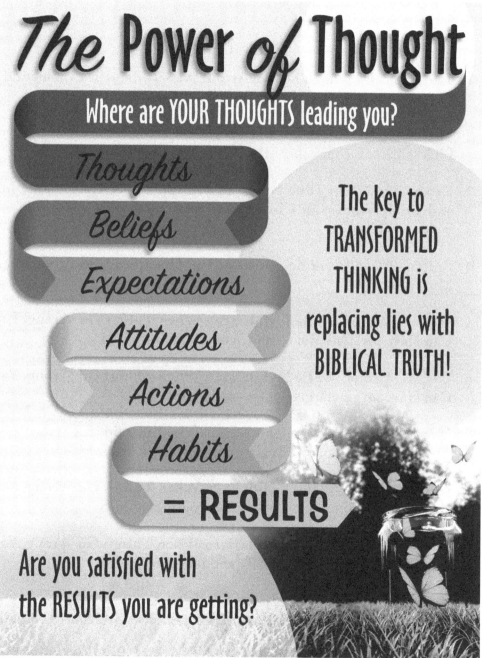

The Power of Thought

Where are YOUR THOUGHTS leading you?

Thoughts

Beliefs

Expectations

Attitudes

Actions

Habits

= RESULTS

The key to TRANSFORMED THINKING is replacing lies with BIBLICAL TRUTH!

Are you satisfied with the RESULTS you are getting?

TRANSFORM MY THINKING, GOD
A Study of the Book of Philippians

ENDNOTES

1 MacArthur Jr., John. **The MacArthur New Testament Commentary Philippians**. Chicago: Moody Press, 2001.

2 "Strong's Exhaustive Bible Concordance Online." *Bible Study Tools*, www. Biblestudytools.com/concordances/strongs-exhaustive-concordance/.

3 Gromacki, Robert. **The Books of Philippians & Colossians: Joy and Completeness in Christ**. Chattanooga: Tyndale Theological Seminary, 2003.

4 Broom, Al & Lorraine. **One to One Discipling**. Multiplication Ministries, 1999.

5 Weirsbe, Warren W. **Be Joyful: Even When Things Go Wrong, You Can Have Joy**. Ontario: Cook Communications, 2005.

6 Weirsbe, Warren W. **Be Joyful: Even When Things Go Wrong, You Can Have Joy**. Ontario: Cook Communications, 2005.

7 Motyer, J. A., and Stott, John R., eds. **The Bible Speaks Today: The Message of Philippians**. England: Inter-Varsity Press, 1984.

8 Weirsbe, Warren W. **Be Joyful: Even When Things Go Wrong, You Can Have Joy**. Ontario: Cook Communications, 2005.

9 Weirsbe, Warren W. **Be Joyful: Even When Things Go Wrong, You Can Have Joy**. Ontario: Cook Communications, 2005.

10 "Strong's Exhaustive Bible Concordance Online." *Bible Study Tools*, www. Biblestudytools.com/concordances/strongs-exhaustive-concordance/.

OTHER RESOURCES USED

Walvoord, John F. and Zuck, Roy B. **The Bible Knowledge Commentary, New Testament Edition**. Cook Communications Ministries, 2004

"Searchable Online Bible with Study Resources." *Blue Letter Bible*, www. blueletterBible.org/.

Elizabeth and Fred Mahusay have a heart for marriages. Every Monday they host a live broadcast called **Marriage Matters Monday**. Be sure to tune in as they share biblically based marriage encouragement!

Visit and Like the 'Rock My Marriage' Facebook page:
www.facebook.com/rockmymarriage

ABOUT THE AUTHOR

A seasoned women's Bible study writer and teacher, Elizabeth enjoys engaging women through God's Word. She has written several other Bible studies including Joshua, Colossians, Ecclesiastes, prayer, and most recently a study equipping women who desire to lead studies. She is currently writing and teaching women at her home church in Allen, TX. She is a passionate, articulate speaker whose life mission is to help all women experience transformational thinking that leads them to impact the world.

Elizabeth graduated with her bachelor's in Chemistry Education and a master's in Instructional Technology from the University of South Florida. She taught high school science for 10 years. Elizabeth married her high school sweetheart, Fred. They have two sons. She has been an entrepreneur for over 16 years and has helped her husband to build his flourishing photography business.